OLD CALIFORNIA HOUSES ⁓

⁓ PORTRAITS AND STORIES

John Bidwell's House, Chico

Old California Houses

← Portraits and Stories

MARION RANDALL PARSONS

BERKELEY AND LOS ANGELES 1952
UNIVERSITY OF CALIFORNIA PRESS

University of California Press
Berkeley and Los Angeles, California

Cambridge University Press
London, England

Copyright, 1952, by
The Regents of the University of California

Designed by John B. Goetz

PREFACE

A painter's quest for subjects was the genesis of this book. The chosen buildings were not necessarily those marked for preservation by the historical societies, nor were the people who had lived or worked or preached in them always those best known to history. As I sketched my way through central California, time and again some shabby old structure, hidden on a narrow city street, at the end of a country lane, on an abandoned farm, or crowning a hill in a mining camp, transformed itself into a symbol of a life and a land familiar to me in childhood and now fast disappearing.

The story of that life—gathered from my memory and from the lips of pioneers as well as from books—could not be confined to dwellings. A shop, a church, a school, a hotel, even a cemetery might yield its contribution. Buildings great or small, of adobe, or frame, or brick, or stone—their fragmentary stories are part of the record of the builders, those men and women whose now forgotten ways of life form the foundation and framework of California history.

M. R. P.

CONTENTS

Part One
A SPANISH NEIGHBORHOOD

    1. Fort Ross, a Count, and a Princess   3
    2. The Petaluma Adobe and General Vallejo   11
    3. Victor Castro's Adobe   20
    4. A Martínez Adobe   29
    5. Rancho Monte del Diablo   39

Part Two
A SCOT, A POLE, AND TWO AMERICANS

    6. The Stone House and John Marsh   51
    7. John Strentzel and John Muir   58
    8. John Bidwell's House   65

Part *Three*

THE FORTY-NINERS TURN RESPECTABLE

    9. A Graveyard and a School   73
    10. Chez Pellaton   81
    11. A Parish Church   87
    12. Bonanza Kelly's Ranch House   94
    13. Napa Soda Springs   100
    14. Woodward's Gardens   106

Part *Four*

THE AGE OF MAGNIFICENCE

    15. Linden Towers and James Clair Flood   113
    16. Adolph Sutro's House   120
    17. Two Queens and Their Castles   126
    Sources   135

ILLUSTRATIONS

John Bidwell's House, Chico
Fort Ross, Sonoma County
General Vallejo's Adobe, Petaluma
Victor Castro's Adobe, San Pablo
A Martínez Adobe, Alhambra Valley
John Marsh's House, near Byron
John Strentzel's and John Muir's House, near Martinez
Schoolhouse and Graveyard, Columbia
Graveyard, Columbia
Pellaton's Store, Mokelumne Hill
St. Canice Church, Nevada City
Bonanza Kelly's House, near Suscol

Napa Soda Springs, Napa County
Woodward's Gardens, San Francisco
James Flood's "Linden Towers," Menlo Park
Adolph Sutro's House, San Francisco
The Hopkins and Stanford Houses, San Francisco

Part One

A SPANISH NEIGHBORHOOD

1. FORT ROSS, A COUNT AND A PRINCESS

On a lonely bluff not many miles north of the mouth of the Russian River, a little Greek chapel built of hand-hewn redwood stands with its back turned to a wide sweep of the Pacific Ocean. Simple as the building looks, crudely primitive, it knew greatness in its day. Generals worshipped there, representatives of a czar in Russia and a king in Spain; a French count, a Russian princess. More clearly than the dwellings of the post, perhaps, or the once sturdy fortress walls, the chapel reflected the spirit of its country and of its times. For only the great of Fort Ross could worship there: the commander, his officers and his guests. Lesser people—the soldiers of the post, the Aleuts, and the California Indians—confronted God in an even cruder chapel, if the word of an old Russian priest who once lived there is to be believed. The exact site of this, near the graveyard, has been lost, for all the buildings in that vicinity burned down in a grass fire many years ago.

The commander of Fort Ross, we are told, during the later years of his tenure lived in some degree of state. The windows of his redwood house were glazed. In the orchard summerhouse, a large enclosure hung with the Russian colors, dinners were served—when the weather permitted. Indeed, a traveler notes, the houses were so elegantly formed and the fields were so well cultivated that the place had a markedly European look: a well-settled look too, in all probability, since the building of the fort had preceded by several years the founding of the first Spanish settlement north of the Golden Gate, Mission San Rafael.

Dates and facts about Bodega and Fort Ross are well documented. The Spanish government's consent to a Russian settlement and the Mexican government's distrust of it; the zeal for otter and seal hunting that outlived the Russians' dwindling enthusiasm for agriculture—these and many more details you may find in any history. But when the story of the short-lived colony turns to that of its most engaging personality, the Princess Helena, authenticated fact ends and legend begins.

Some few facts about her, and many of the side lights, come from the ready pen of Count Eugène Duflot de Mofras, that John Gunther of the 1840's whose nine months' tour of Alta California, from San Diego to Vancouver, encouraged him to write with authority on California's botany, geology, agriculture, and Indian philology, and to draw topographical and geographical maps. He was an attaché of the French legation in Mexico City, commissioned by his government to make a report on Alta California and the doings of the nations most actively interested in its future, England, in particular. He was a talented and cultivated young man, not devoid of charm. Even General Vallejo, who hated him on sight, admitted that he could be a gentleman when he chose. That De Mofras's statements and conclusions are not wholly reliable is not altogether his fault. Vallejo's brother Salvador, displeased at the Frenchman's rather arrogant manner and persistent questioning, tricked him into writing an account of the nonexistent Santa Rosa Mission and the growing of vanilla in its luxuriant herb gardens. De Mofras's blunders, however, seem unimportant as compared with the revealing glimpses he gives of little things that so many travel writers neglect. Although he records the dimensions of the stockade and blockhouses of the fort, he does not forget to tell us that the Greek chapel is "surmounted by a cross and pleasant little bells." Nor do dull figures about population and trade crowd out his interest in the church's interior: its pictures in jeweled frames, its ornaments of silver and gold. No doubt Princess Helena interested him even more.

She was the daughter of the Prince de Gagarin, a nobleman of distinguished family, if not, as is sometimes held, a cousin or niece of the czar. A blonde, exquisite, brilliant, and amiable, she possessed the added and, in Alta California quite unprecedented, attraction of a Parisian wardrobe. She had married Baron Alexander Rotcheff, the last commander at

Fort Ross—eloped with him, George Lyman rather grumpily asserts—and had come to share his not too unhappy isolation on the wild and lonely California coast. Another grudging commentator concedes that she is reputed to have been clever as well as attractive. De Mofras gives the clearest picture of all in a few urbane sentences that do not even mention her name. "Fort Ross with its gardens has a superb location . . . Anyone who has led the terrible life of a trapper . . . or has been pursued by the yells of savages can fully appreciate the joy of a choice library, French wines, a piano, and a score of Mozart."

It seems ungracious to belittle Count Eugène's wild frontier experiences. But since he journeyed for the most part by sea and was accorded every travel facility that the times would permit, and since the northern frontier under Vallejo's rule is said to have been the most orderly and safe part of all California, his hardships perhaps were not greater than those of another traveler in that period who wrote that his hosts had shown him to a magnificent bed, adorned with embroidered spread and sheets—but the Indian servants had forgotten blankets, and he had to shiver through the night as best he could. It is amusing to recall that thirty years later, in a letter to Bancroft, De Mofras, unable to recall more personal travel incidents than those published in his book, urges in defense, "je voyais sans cesse des ours dans le forêt.

De Mofras's sufferings included a dance in honor of Princess Helena's birthday—or perhaps the word "hardship" is again more apt—for the dance lasted a week. On another occasion a party of thirty journeyed from Sonoma to a Russian farm near Bodega. They started in the morning, arrived at evening, danced all night and the following night, and on the third day started home at sunrise. Count Eugène does not say, specifically, that the Princess devoted the whole three days to this lusty sport; but other evidence shows that she was a lively and enterprising young woman, not content to limit her California experience to the luxurious surroundings of Fort Ross.

Of the most notable of her adventures—the exploration and naming of Mount Saint Helena in June, 1841—no clear account has come down to us. Some sources credit the scientist Vosnesensky with the first ascent and the naming of the mountain in honor of the Czarina. Others give that honor to Princess Helena, and indeed embroider the occasion with considerable detail. Yet we are still left in doubt whether she really did ascend the mountain herself, with husband, scientists and soldiers in attendance; whether she stood with arm aloft invoking the Holy Trinity while her retinue knelt at her feet; whether the mountain was climbed on the saint's day and named for the saint with the Princess graciously concurring; and whether the Indian chief, Solano, really did capture the whole party at the foot of the mountain and hold it in duress until an always gallant general came to the rescue. Or was the true story something entirely different?

That Mariano Guadalupe Vallejo had at least a hand in the episode is beyond doubt. His version of the incident—other versions suggest that his memory of details was not always accurate—can best be given in a translation (by Nellie Van de Grift Sanchez) of his own bombastic words:

"When Señor Rotcheff . . . came to see me, he was accompanied by his wife, the Princess Elena, a very beautiful lady of twenty Aprils, who united to her other gifts an irresistible affability. The beauty of the governor's wife made such a deep impression on the heart of Chief Solano that he conceived the project of stealing her. With this object he came to visit me very late at night and asked my consent to putting his plan into effect. The story horrified me, for if it should unfortunately be carried out my good name would suffer, for no one would be able to get it out of his head that my agent had acted on my account; and besides seeing the country involved in a war provoked by the same cause which actuated the siege of Troy, I, who had never hesitated at expense or trouble to please my visitors, . . . would be stigmatized as the most disloyal being that the world had ever produced. It was necessary for me to assume all the authority that I knew how to assume on occasions that required it to make Solano understand that his life would hang in the balance if he should be so ill-advised as to attempt to break the rules of hospitality. My words produced a good effect, and that same night, repenting of his conduct, he went to Napa Valley, where I sent him to prevent him from compromising, under the impulse of his insane love, the harmony which it was so urgent for me to reestablish with my powerful neighbors . . . But, fear-ing that Solano might ambush them on the road, I went to escort my visitors to Bodega."

The translator, with that touch of acidity that the beauty of the Princess seemed wont to provoke, adds: "As for the lady, like the coquette that she probably was, she expressed herself as enchanted with the adventure, and especially with having been rescued from the splendid savage by such cavaliers."

In accounts by other chroniclers, Vallejo is not given so prominent a part. But the valiant General liked life to be on the grand scale, and the incident seems to have impressed him deeply. Elsewhere he mentions having kissed the Princess' hand in parting, and says that he has always remembered her beauty and graciousness with the greatest pleasure. However, he adds, the occurrence has never been regarded with equal satisfaction by his wife.

We hear little more of Princess Helena. Yet when Gertrude Atherton visited Fort Ross half a century later, her name was still green. An old half-breed woman had further legendary matter to gossip about. The Princess had not been altogether happy at Ross. On occasion she had even been haunted. There had been "apparitions of red-headed dwarfs" who "did not appear to have any object in swarming beyond . . . frightening people half to death, particularly the Princess, who had no use for them whatever." There were traditions of other ghosts, and of murders. "A man of the 'town' once flung his wife over the cliffs . . . Another wife went over on her own account, doubtless preferring to keep the initiative." There were cruel floggings, executions.

In spite of its reported elegance, life at Fort Ross must have been in reality as rough and brutal as life in any other frontier community. It is said, however, that the Russians were exceptionally good to the Indians: that they paid them for their lands, even if only with beads and simple tools; that they taught them crafts without trying to Christianize them. And, strangely enough, the Indians liked the way the Russians treated them. No Indian attacks upon the Russians have been reported; and Vallejo's later success in handling Indian problems, as against earlier difficulties, may have resulted from shrewd observations of Russian tactics on his several visits to Fort Ross.

In any event, the Princess must have rejoiced when the imperial orders came to withdraw from California. A hard journey lay ahead: up the coast to Sitka, across Bering Strait, then three to five months of winter travel across Siberia to Moscow in large sleighs lined inside with wolfskins and curtained against the icy winds. In the face of this and unmentioned hardships that can well be imagined, De Mofras managed to give the story a happy ending:

"Recently Princess Hélène . . . departed on this long journey without fear."

2. THE PETALUMA ADOBE AND GENERAL VALLEJO

The old adobe fort that overlooks the Petaluma Valley was built in 1834, a time when the Russian settlement at Fort Ross was giving the rulers of Alta California some concern. Whether in the interest of counteracting the influence of these insidious foreigners, or of furthering Mexican settlement, Vallejo was given charge of the "northern frontier"—all the country north of the Bay, the area now included in Marin, Sonoma, Lake, and Solano counties. His task was to pacify the very fierce and belligerent Indian tribes, to found the pueblo of Sonoma, and to inveigle Mexicans into settling in the fertile valleys. And he was successful in all these enterprises.

The fort—or the Palace, or the Casa Grande, as it has also been called—has, unhappily, not been preserved as one of California's historic landmarks. It is fast falling into ruin. And a house just outside the town of Sonoma, the last of several dwellings built by Mariano Guadalupe Vallejo in the county in which most of his life was spent, has been awarded landmark honors instead. Lachryma Montis, a prim, conventional, early Victorian house, gabled and fretworked and furnished with round-backed, uncomfortable, formerly horsehair-covered chairs, indeed well represents his latter days, the forty years of life still left to him after he built it in 1850. It is the proper setting for the elderly man of his most familiar photographs: portly, stately, a "gentleman of fine presence and arrogant ways." These words, used by him to describe the detested Count Eugène, apply equally well to Vallejo. He was side-whiskered, pompous, sure of his own rightness, though with a genial side to him too, which found expression in an extravagant hospitality. Yet among the voluminous pages that Mariano Guadalupe wrote about California and about himself another character lurks. There is an engaging naïveté about this less publicized young man, which is best reflected, not by Lachryma Montis with its fifty-six servants, its orchestra of harp, violin, flute, and guitar, its roster of famous guests, but by that much earlier adobe fort.

When the construction of the adobe began, Vallejo was still very young. His marriage to Francisca Benicia Carrillo, a "spinster of fifteen" whom he had met at her home in San Diego, had taken place only two years before. Writing of his courtship some half century later, Vallejo says that he had never seen a young lady "more earnestly in love." The courtship had prospered. The parents on both sides had given consent. But as an officer in the Mexican army, Mariano, before he could marry, had to have permission from the Minister of War in Mexico City.

The petition was duly dispatched by "slow burro express"; but what with donkey recalcitrance, messenger aversion to hurry, and official reluctance to commit a decision to paper, the longed-for *permiso* was delayed for a year and a half. Immediately upon its arrival, the wedding took place in San Diego in the presence of Governor Echeandía and all his staff. But at supper the governor ended his speech of congratulation with the news that the bridegroom was to be at once sent on a military expedition to the north. The bridal pair "shuddered," yet maintained the proper composure and "allowed no one to see the affliction of their hearts." Dancing persisted until six in the morning, and before the guests dispersed, Vallejo's orders came. He writes: "Transport yourself mentally to those times . . . Twenty-four years of age, full of dreams, an ardent soul, abounding health! Alas, just . . . when I believed that there did not exist . . . a more enviable being than I . . . a cruel hand broke the cup from which I was about to drink the nectar of my happiness . . ."

Eight months elapsed, Vallejo tells us, before he and his bride met again; for after his campaign he was made *comandante* of the presidio of San Francisco and director of colonization. Because he could not leave his post, he sent his brother Salvador with twenty troopers to bring his bride from San Diego. Their son, Dr. Platón Vallejo, goes on with the story: "My mother never wearied telling of this journey. The soldiers were all young, very striking in their new uniforms. An easy-paced jack . . . was assigned for her to ride. She was seated on a sort of pillion, and, instead of a stirrup her feet rested on a board suspended along the jack's side. It was no more tiresome than sitting in a rocking chair. One of the soldiers held the bridle, and, except at night, never relaxed his grasp from San Diego to San Francisco. . . . It was in spring time. All the country was carpeted with flowers . . . Sometimes they stayed over night at the Missions . . . But more often they camped by some limpid stream . . . and in the morning she was awakened by the birds singing their own wedding march."

A romantic story, but far from accurate if a later historian is to be believed. At the wedding, duty called not to a campaign but to a council of war in San Diego, after which Vallejo returned to his bride and spent some months with her. And the record would seem to substantiate the charge that the General, writing so long after the event, was indeed a little hazy about the facts. For the wedding took place on March 6, 1832, and the first child was born in San Francisco on March 4, 1833! At least the journey on the jackass is left for fancy to play with.

Vallejo's Petaluma house was the most imposing adobe dwelling in northern California. Today it is little more than half its original size, for the whole south wing was destroyed by fire years ago. The building seems to have been used rather rarely as a private home. The Vallejo family spent holiday times there, and it was always kept equipped to entertain travelers or an overflow of guests if the General's other big adobe, near the mission in the pueblo of Sonoma, could hold no more. It was a garrison at times, but above all else a huge workshop. It fed and housed six hundred laborers and vaqueros, and every morning, in the great inner courtyard, roll was called before the workers set about the task of the day. There was probably more than a hint of the military in this daily ceremony, for Vallejo was a stickler for discipline. On a visit to Santa Barbara in 1839 he was so shocked to find junior officers addressing Governor Alvarado, his nephew, as Juanito, and General Castro as José, that he took drastic measures. Within a few days, practically every officer at the post was under arrest. When General Castro himself was arrested for failing to arrest other offenders, Vallejo at last saw the absurdity of trying to maintain strict discipline in an army officered by relatives—moreover, an army serving virtually without pay.

Vallejo's own military career had begun when he was fifteen. Before that he had been a clerk to William Hartnell in Monterey. From him he had learned French, some English, and the rudiments of trade. Whatever the great Spanish landowners may have become in the American period, in earlier times they were not idlers. Every "educated young gentleman was well skilled in many arts and handicrafts," Guadalupe Vallejo (Mariano's niece) asserts. At his Petaluma hacienda, Vallejo had need of all he had learned: tanning, weaving, soapmaking, wheat growing. The wheat was marketed to the Russians, who had mysteriously been transformed from menace to a highly profitable outlet for Petaluma wares. Vallejo knew how to cut out and put together a pair of shoes, roll cigars, make candles, burn lime, tan hides, and make bricks, as well as to plan a campaign or read Telemaco.

His interest in reading at one time involved him, together with two boon companions of his young days, José Castro and Juan Bautista Alvarado, in difficulties with the church. In 1831 the trio bought a cargo of forbidden books that had arrived on a Mexican vessel. Through Castro's sweetheart, it is said, the news of their sinful studies reached the ears of Father Durán, prelate of the missions. He demanded surrender of the books. The youths refused to give them up, and were promptly excommunicated. They did not, however, allow that to interfere with their reading. Eventually, Alvarado, who had possession of some money due Father Durán, went to him, saying that since any dealings with an excommunicate would bring excommunication on Father Durán too, unhappily no money could pass between them. The padre thereupon explained that the young men were suffering under a minor, not a major, excommunication, and that he had power to annul the sentence. This he did. Alvarado thanked the priest, paid the money, stayed to lunch—and the youths went on reading whatever they liked.

In their later years Alvarado was not always on such friendly terms with his Uncle Mariano. This was not only, one suspects, because of political differences. Vallejo's strong sense of propriety must often have been offended by his nephew's lesser dignity. Brilliant and gifted though Juan Bautista Alvarado unquestionably was, it was said that his marriage by proxy had not been occasioned by pressure of affairs, but that illness resulting from a heavy drinking bout had prevented him from attending his own wedding. Jealousy of the young governor's wit and ability may have been another factor in Vallejo's displeasure. The pungency of Juan Bautista's prose as against Mariano's prolixity points their differences. The policy of emperor and clergy, Alvarado says, has been to make *burros de carga* of the people. They should have known that this won't serve with republicans. Sooner or later the "ass was sure to kick."

Among the accounts of the many political dissensions, quarrels with friends, and financial difficulties that darken the story of Vallejo's middle life it is pleasant to read of his fast friendship with the Indian chief Sem Yet, better known by his baptismal name, Francisco Solano. All the Vallejos seem to have held the Indian in very high esteem. And if through their paeans of praise a whisper penetrates—Solano sometimes rather ran amuck in his religious observances; Solano planned the kidnapping not only of a foreign princess but also of some of his own compatriots—there is no doubt that he was a valuable ally at a time when the warring tribes threatened the whole project of settlement. Beyond all question he was devoted heart and soul to Vallejo. At the time of the Bear Flag episode, when Vallejo was arrested by Frémont's men and imprisoned at Sutter's Fort, Solano disappeared. For twelve years nothing was known of his fate. Then one day, without warning, he reappeared at Lachryma Montis. Believing that Vallejo had been killed in the uprising, he had fled to the north. In his wanderings he had even penetrated far into British Columbia. While Solano was away his wife continued to live on the Vallejo estate, and there, after his return, he too remained until his death.

After the American conquest, Vallejo lived quietly on his Sonoma estate, no longer lord of the whole northern frontier, yet feeling himself still official host in all that part of California. Sometimes there were so many guests that the three tortilla makers had to be augmented to five. His stately manner of living must, he felt, be maintained at any cost. Once when a chance visitor came upon him working in his garden, Vallejo hastily summoned his secretary. Monsieur Prudon was instructed to escort the stranger to the General's office. Vallejo then disappeared by way of the back door and a few minutes later emerged in state—by the front door, one infers—wearing his best uniform and epaulettes.

Vallejo founded, or helped to found, cities—Benicia, named for his wife, Vallejo named for himself—in the vain hope that the metropolis of the Bay region and the capitol of California would be located in the "central" region of San Pablo Bay. He was not without honor among the Americans, though at times, among his less courtly new associates, his proud dignity subjected him to some ridicule. As a member of the constitutional convention in Monterey in 1848, disturbed at finding a bear in the proposed state emblem, he suggested that the animal be shown securely held by a lariat in the hands of a vaquero. This recommendation was voted down with laughter that must have bitterly wounded him. Nonetheless, the ball that ended the convention was one of his great social triumphs, a climax in his career.

As a senator in the first session of the state legislature he was chairman of a committee appointed to report on the derivation of county names, a committee on which General Bidwell also served. At Lachryma Montis he entertained Sherman, Sheridan, Farragut, and on his own visit to Washington he was received by President Lincoln. Two of his daughters married the sons of a Hungarian nobleman. Yet the years became increasingly clouded. He lost title to the Soscol rancho, lost numberless acres of Sonoma and Petaluma lands to squatters, and never recovered the money poured out for the city of Vallejo. He even had to sell the great Petaluma hacienda. He spent his later years writing his *Historia* and assembling the priceless Spanish Californian documents that still bear his name.

"I have had my day; it was a proud one," he once said.

3. VICTOR CASTRO'S ADOBE

The date when the earliest dwelling on the San Pablo grant was built is still a matter of conjecture. The first shelter was of "palizada type"—that is, it was made of redwood posts thrust into the ground, walled and roofed with tules and hides—and was used perhaps only by vaqueros. A low building adjoining the two-story adobe on San Pablo Avenue in El Cerrito that for a century has been known as Victor Castro's home is thought to be one of several adobes built by his father, Don Francisco Castro, to house his family. Just south of the group of buildings, Cerrito Creek divided Castro lands from those of the Peraltas.

All of the country east of San Francisco Bay, rather vaguely designated as the Contra Costa ("the opposite shore"), long remained remote and uninhabited. Pedro Fages, who had been a member of the Portolá expedition, which had blundered into knowledge of San Francisco Bay and its outlet to the sea in 1769, visited this eastern shore briefly in 1770. In the early spring of 1772, with Father Juan Crespi and twelve soldiers, he again explored northward from Monterey Bay. After crossing the Salinas River and traversing the Santa Clara Valley, they marched along the eastern shore of San Francisco Bay, over the sites of the present towns of San Leandro, Oakland, Berkeley and Martinez, and round Suisun Bay to the mouth of the San Joaquin River. This, to add to the confusion of geographers, Father Crespi named the Rio de San Francisco. Perhaps the great sheet of water now honored with the good saint's name was shrouded in fog when Fages passed along its shores, for it was San Pablo Bay that won from him the admiring observation that it was deep and large enough to hold all the armadas of Spain.

San Pablo Point, San Pedro Point opposite it, and Carquinez Strait all are early names, dating from 1811 or even before. Later, about 1828, Pinole ("cereal meal") commemorates soldier satisfaction in a mess of pottage, as the near-by Cañada del Hambre ("glade of hunger") records an occasion when a band of soldiers, out of provisions, lamented the lack of any such feast. In these early years, however, except for accounts of minor explorations or expeditions in pursuit of Indians, the Contra Costa is seldom mentioned in history.

About the time of the founding of Mission San Rafael (1817) the San Pablo area appears in the records as a grazing ground for sheep and cattle belonging to Mission Dolores. A large part of this pastureland, north of that granted to Don Luis Peralta in

1820, was granted three years later to Don Francisco Castro. In a letter published in the *Contra Costa Gazette* of July 7, 1860, Pablo Antonio María Castro, the eldest son of Don Francisco, asserts that his father came across the bay, from Olompali, and took possession of the lands "about the year 1814," an earlier date than any in the records I have seen. Possibly Don Francisco's coming over and his taking possession were separate occurrences, spaced by several years. In any event, with the exception of those of the Peraltas, the Castro holdings preceded all others on the Contra Costa.

Don Francisco was born in Sinaloa in 1775, and before coming to the East Bay had served as a soldier in the San Francisco presidio and later as alcalde of the pueblo of San José. His family is said to have been in California since 1784. The name Macario Castro appears in early Monterey records and also at San Juan Bautista, later the headquarters of that turbulent grandson of his, José Castro, who contributed rather more than his share to the confusion of petty wars and revolutions that clutter the history of California's Mexican period. No land grant is recorded in Macario's name, but he and his descendants are credited with having contributed much to the building of missions and presidios and pueblos. The relationship of Francisco's family to that of Macario is not clear, though an incident mentioned later suggests that some connection did exist.

The account of a visitor to Rancho San Pablo in 1827, Auguste Bernard du Hautcilly, indicates that it was then a thriving home; building operations must therefore have begun considerably earlier. Today it is hard for us to realize that the crudest adobe with earthen floors, unglazed windows, and without fireplace or chimney, represented a second phase, an advance over first primitive conditions. For adobe bricks had to be mixed, shaped, dried; they were not formed into houses in a day.

Monsieur Duhaut-Cilly (as his name is usually written) tells us that Francisco Castro was a "worthy man" who "was descended from a Frenchman who has left in California a large and estimable family. At eleven we arrived at the beach nearest the farm where two of Castro's sons awaited us with horses. The friendliest reception was prepared for us in this truly patriarchal dwelling. Francisco Castro was a man of sixty years [fifty-three according to other records], of noble face and figure and perfectly preserved. His entire family, comprising ten children and two daughters-in-law, lived under the same roof in perfect harmony . . ."

The French visitor possibly did not know that harmony, in Spanish families of that period, was rather rigorously imposed. A visitor to another household describes a breakfast table with papa seated at the end imbibing his chocolate while ranks of grown-up sons and daughters stand at attention behind him. When they left the room, whether hungry or fed is not stated, they kissed the old man's hand as they filed past.

Duhaut-Cilly goes on to tell us that while he was there two of the Castro sons went on a bear hunt. He himself apparently dodged active participation in this genteel sport, but he relates that, although the young men returned with two bear cubs, one son, while on horseback, had been attacked by the mother bear. Duhaut-Cilly adds plaintively that they merely joked about it, and "Castro, who loved his children to distraction, hardly seemed to ·notice they had almost been torn by the claws of this terrible adversary."

These sons—and daughters—of Francisco Castro contribute their own special brand of confusion to the chaotic annals of these early times. Francisco died in 1831, four years before his temporary grant was confirmed to his heirs. The heirs, however, after the confirmation of the grant, were far from satisfied with the way the terms of Francisco's will had worked out. He had bequeathed half of his property to his widow, Gabriela Berryessa de Castro, and the other half to his ten children. Three of these, daughters, had died without issue, leaving their shares to their mother, who in turn had inconsiderately been inspired to deed all of her property to daughter Martina, the wife of Governor Juan Bautista Alvarado. Martina therefore, if my authority's arithmetic is not at fault, by her mother's contrivance owned fifteen twenty-seconds of the entire estate, whereas her father had meant her to have only a tenth part of half of it. Naturally, ructions ensued. The other heirs tried to break Francisco's will, years after his death. The title to the property became so involved that no son or daughter could know what really was his. And as for living together in harmony—all one can report on this point is that sons Victor and Juan José are said to have built the two-story adobe that still stands on San Pablo Avenue near

Cerrito Creek, and son Jesús María built a new home, three or four miles away on Wildcat Creek, for Gabriela, his mother. When Martina and Juan Bautista Alvarado went there to live with her in 1848 it was "still new and unfinished." After Gabriela Castro died in 1851, the Alvarados made her adobe their permanent home. It, too, is still standing in the present town of San Pablo. Although only a hundred feet or so from the highway, it is so well hidden by stores and cottages that not one motorist in a thousand knows that it is there. Gone are the famous grape arbors and the gardens and orchards that once surrounded it. Nothing green is left except one big weeping willow.

The names of Francisco Castro's sons occur quite frequently in local annals. Bancroft says, "In early troubles with the Indians as well as in later contests with the squatters, Don Victor has repeatedly shown himself to be a brave and determined man." Victor raised cattle and vegetables. He owned a schooner-launch and a whaleboat. He and his young companions used to cross the Bay on Sunday mornings to attend church at San Rafael, and he often carried passengers to festivals in Yerba Buena. His boats also served to ferry passengers between Yerba Buena and Sausalito and Sonoma. He was always kind and obliging, William Heath Davis tells us: he entertained passengers as his guests if there was any delay about the boats, and he and his beautiful wife Luisa were graciousness itself. His landing at Cerritos was habitually used until Semple's ferry at Benicia, which advertised a boat "waiting at either end for the convenience of travelers," and the steam ferry up San Antonio Creek came into being along with other Yankee innovations.

The difficulties of travel that the early rancheros experienced are hard to realize today. In 1835, thirty landowners from the Contra Costa petitioned the government in Monterey to remove the East Bay area from the jurisdiction of San Francisco and place it under the jurisdiction of San José. "To go to the port [of San Francisco] by land, we are under the necessity of traveling forty leagues . . . and to go by sea we are exposed to the danger of being wrecked." Under certain conditions it was almost impossible to travel by land at all. The clumsy wooden-wheeled *carretas* could not get through the winter mud. There were no bridges. As late as 1839 a bridal party of thirty people on their way from Pinole to Mission San José had to cross San Leandro, San Lorenzo, and Alameda creeks at a time of very high water. On their return, they found San Leandro Creek in flood, and had to camp on its banks for several days. It is to be hoped that the sun was shining and musicians were not wanting, so that the wedding festivities were not interrupted, but merely prolonged. Brides, happily, did not ride in *carretas*; according to the ritual that prevailed in the best families, the bride rode on horseback, with the godfather behind her on the horse's haunches on the way to church, and the bridegroom in that far from lordly position on the way home.

These early families of course all intermarried. Victor Castro became the husband of Luisa Martínez, a daughter of Don Ignacio Martínez on the neighboring Rancho Pinole. Although they too may have been "earnestly in love," their marriage perhaps was influenced by certain practical considerations. In 1838, General Vallejo sent out a sergeant and ten soldiers to pick up recruits among the unmarried men in his vicinity. A young neighbor got wind of this enterprise, rode across the hills to Soscol, and thence crossed Carquinez Strait—perhaps on one of the tule rafts that one reads about, on which the passenger sat in the water and paddled himself across—to warn Victor Castro. Victor in turn rode to warn a young Martínez, who was about his own age, fifteen, and the two galloped off to the haven of San Juan Bautista, then under the command of General José Castro, who is said to have been a relative of Victor. Perhaps it was on the advice of this rival general that the boys both were married the next year.

The Castro sons had tangled with Vallejo even before 1838, if various chroniclers are to be believed. Probably there is some foundation for the story, though the dates given make Victor thirteen at the time of the first incident, and this casts some doubt on its accuracy. Three of the brothers, it was said, Joaquín, Antonio, and Victor, trading with the Indians around Santa Rosa, carried off several to San Pablo to work for them. Vallejo arrested the trio and sent them to Monterey for punishment. Two years later, the same three were involved in a plot designed to weaken Vallejo's hold on the frontier. They carried Peruvian liquor to Soscol and got Chief Solano so drunk that he helped them kidnap still more Indian children—for which he afterward did heavy penance to Vallejo, who had taken a strong stand against this abuse of the Indians. The story would shock us more were it not for the fact that the enlightened American people did not get around to endorsing the good General's views on the bartering of human beings until thirty years later, and that the shanghaiing of sailors continued far longer.

It is easy to believe that the sons of that worthy man Don Francisco Castro were masters of a kindly sort. A chapel for the Indians was maintained on the rancho for many years. Indeed, Rancho San Pablo must have been a happy place in the days of growing prosperity that preceded the Mexican War. Food was plentiful. The hardships of frontier living had given way to greater comfort and peace. One should not be misled by the sinister gloom that darkens Victor Castro's old adobe today. The evil look it now wears may well be merely an emanation from its recent sordid history. Used as night club and gambling den, surrounded by a dog racecourse, street fairs, junk shops, trailer camps, the old house now stands in empty desolation, facing the most squalid and unsightly aspects of our current civilization. One may be forgiven if, when driving along San Pablo Avenue, one breathes a nostalgic sigh for days when the big family lived there in harmony and could ride through leagues of flower fields to meet the rare traveler or chase the abundant bear.

4. A MARTINEZ ADOBE

When Doña Encarnación Martínez married Don Abelino Altamirano, the wedding festivities lasted all summer. The guests, neighbors for fifty miles around, camped under the oaks and sycamores along Baca Creek and, in the intervals of singing and dancing and feasting, fashioned bricks and erected walls. When autumn came, the little dwelling in the Cañada del Hambre stood complete.

So, at least, to this day, old people tell the legend in the Alhambra Valley. A charming idyl, it seems a pity to cast doubt upon its authenticity. Yet the facts seem to be that Encarnación's adobe was not built in her father's lifetime, and she was married some years before Don Ignacio died. Her house, on land now a part of the Swett Ranch, is still lived in, yet it is so well hidden in woods beyond Baca Creek that many people now living on neighboring ranches have never seen it. Her brother Vicente's adobe, on the other hand, a mile or more away on the John Strentzel (later the Muir) ranch, is one of the well-known landmarks of the near-by town of Martinez.

Don Ignacio Martínez was one of the earliest rancheros on the Contra Costa, indeed one of California's first pioneers. He became an officer in the Spanish army, and later served in the Mexican army. Having been sent to the San Francisco Presidio about 1817, he later served for many years as its *comandante*. "He abhorred the place, and strove by all means to get himself transferred," one unnamed commentator observes, and adds in malice, "he never did, though!"

Don Ignacio sometimes made enemies, it would appear. A member of the Galindo family is said to have called him a sanguinary despot; and General Vallejo records his own smug conviction that certain misfortunes suffered by Don Ignacio may be regarded as a divine punishment for sundry sins. José Arnaz, on the contrary, found him "most polite, merry, and fond of dances." And who should know better than Arnaz, for he had visited Don Ignacio some fifty times and he couldn't remember a night when they hadn't had a ball. Duhaut-Cilly had certain difficult moments with Don Ignacio, and in his book grows very heated on the subject of a proper anchorage for his vessel. Yet when he paid his respects in due form to Don Ignacio in the house of the *comandante* at the Presidio, he was given a "fort obligeant accueil."

This visitor was enchanted to find that his host's large family included "many young girls of very pleasing appearance." They plied him with tortillas, cheese, cakes and wine. Of these young Californians he says, "Their bloom, their liveliness hardly restrained by the presence of strangers, pleased us." He further notes that when the guns of his vessel saluted Don Ignacio the added "empressement" with which the pretty daughters served him seemed to say, "Papa must be a very great man, since they fire seven guns in his honor."

There was, indeed, no lack of pretty girls in Don Ignacio's home. In 1841 he lists six unmarried daughters, from Encarnación, who is thirty-three, to Dolores, who is ten; and in his application to Governor Alvarado for new grant papers to replace the original document of 1823 which had been lost, he says he needs land, "to comply with the wants of a large family that God has given to me." There were sons, too, José de Jesús Ciriaco and Vicente; and tradition has it that, until his death, Don Ignacio, like his neighbor Don Francisco, kept all his children, married or single, living under his own eye.

He had moved his family in 1837 from San José, where he had served as alderman and lieutenant of militia, to the Rancho el Pinole—sometimes called the Rancho de la Merced, after the religious order of which Ignacio's brother was a member. It was a wild and remote valley, as William Heath Davis describes it, with high encircling hills. Herds of elk grazed there, along with the cattle. There had been a palizada dwelling on the land as early as 1828, somewhat east of the town of Pinole, according to Dr. Bowman. An existing photograph, taken not many years ago, shows a ruined wall and a single window frame—all that was then left of the principal house. Now even those are gone; the adobe bricks have dissolved again into soil, and no living member of the family can identify the site.

It is said that Don Ignacio's eldest son, Don José, from a very early time lived on the rancho like one of his vaqueros, enduring much hardship and privation. Indeed, even after the house was built and the family established there, living conditions could have been none too easy. "His [Don Ignacio's] life was not the gay, irresponsible life of the California ranchero Prince, but that of a hard-working official who retired from military and civilian life only when he had to. To his children belonged the princely life, for a while."

It is possible that the housebuilding was not completed until after the family moved in, for in that same year, on the occasion of the marriage of Don José de Jesús to a daughter of the Peraltas, Don Ignacio, so the story runs, had to add extra rooms to accommodate all the guests. It seems more likely that the added units were designed not for hospitality but rather to house the newly married pair and the brothers and sisters who, with all their spouses, were to live for a decade to come in lesser adobes clustered round the parental dwelling like baby chicks about the mother hen. But the occasion of Don José's marriage was undoubtedly splendid. There were picnics, bullfights, feats of horsemanship. One was expected to dance all night, and only the three hours after sunrise could be given to sleep. The week-long festivities ended only when the hundred guests were completely exhausted.

José de Jesús by all accounts must have been the

young Spanish *caballero* at his charming, generous, high-spirited best. His portrait, cherished by one of his descendants, shows a fine-featured, very handsome man, kindly, dignified. He was only forty-six when he died in the early 'sixties. His funeral, William Heath Davis tells us, was attended by hundreds, who came in "wagons, buggies and carriages"—the vehicles of José's era, as against the oxcarts in the funeral procession that had followed Don Ignacio's coffin from Pinole to Mission San José in 1848.

The younger son, Vicente José Ramón, is better known to Californians of today, though his is a somewhat vicarious fame. It rests, in the main, on another portrait, one not kept among the family treasures but hanging in San Francisco's City Hall. Among that city's distinguished mayors, Ignacio Martínez unquestionably has a place. A portrait enshrined on the wall and labeled with his name shows a round-cheeked, cheery-looking man of middle age, with sideburns and turned-down white collar and black bow tie. "But that's not Ignacio—it's Vicente!" a member of the family once exclaimed, and further pointed out to the official in attendance that Ignacio had long clung to the fashion of wearing his hair in a queue. Moreover, since on his honorable retirement from forty-one years of military service Ignacio had been accorded the privilege not only of collecting full pay but also of continuing to wear his uniform, a portrait of him certainly would have shown him in full panoply. "Oh!" said the dismayed official. "Oh dear me! But you see, ma'am—he's all we've got!" And so Vicente continues to hang there in his father's name.

Vicente's two-story adobe still stands, as good as new, on land that eventually became a part of the John Strentzel ranch. Family records make it quite certain that until after Ignacio's death neither Vicente nor his sister Encarnación could have owned any part of their father's grant or could have begun any building for themselves. Indeed, both adobes are generally attributed to the late 'forties, or, more specifically, to 1849. No date has been found for Encarnación's marriage, nor any clue to the surprising fact that a reigning belle was still unmarried at thirty-three. Her husband, too, remains something of a mystery. In Bancroft's list of pioneers, Abelino Altamirano is included, with the bald statement, "at Los Angeles, 1846." Another Altamirano, Justo Roberto, came to California in very early days, for he was a soldier of the Anza expedition. Some of his younger children were born in San Francisco and Santa Clara. The family may have been among America's Very Very First, for a Lieutenant Juan Altamirano served with Cortes in 1541. I have seen a deed which was signed by Abelino with a cross, his name being written by someone else—an inability to write one's name was not unusual in a society that conspicuously lacked schools. That seems to be all that is known of him.

And of Encarnación? Stories about the women in Spanish families are hard to find. Their names appear rarely in the records. Their proper occupations, comments Brigida Briones, were said to be "dancing, music, religion, and amiability." A few interesting portraits have come down to us, notably one of Vallejo's mother and one of Don Ignacio's wife. They are alike in the way that portraits of early Bostonian women are alike—in that they express a common purposiveness and austerity and strength. They have sad faces, these older women of the Spanish aristocracy, but there is no flabbiness in them, no self pity. They could assert themselves quite forcefully at need. Vallejo is said to have been in terror of his mother to the end of her life. And as for that Doña María Martina Ramírez de Arellano who married Ignacio Martínez, it is related of her that she once took a horsewhip to a grown son when he displeased her in his choice of a wife. And when her son-in-law José de los Santos de Berryessa destroyed Ignacio's will, he swore in court that Doña Martina had been the moving spirit in that act of "justice" toward younger children deprived of certain anticipations by the bequest to the eldest son, who, Don Ignacio had held, was entitled to a larger share of the estate because of his years of privation.

We hear something of the sisters—of María, who married the enterprising sailor, William A. Richardson, and of Susana, whose second husband was William M. Smith. Smith had been a circus rider in Mexico, William Heath Davis claims. He was a dangerous man when the drink was in him; and though he "could assume the manner and air of a gentleman," yet "through all the superficial polish the circus rider was discernible." After Don Ignacio's death, Smith acted as agent for the estate, and he is credited with having had no small part in the founding of the town of Martinez. In 1854 he committed suicide, being "fond of using his pistol," Davis explains.

Of Encarnación little more is known, and that by

legend mostly. Some ageless quality about her seems to have caught men's fancy and kept her name alive. She was very beautiful, they say, the most beautiful perhaps of all the pretty sisters who in earlier years had charmed the French traveler at the Presidio. She was noted for her gaiety and spirit and had been a great belle in her day. Perhaps in her lonely valley she could not live down the memory of that or resign herself to the life of piety that—so her stern mother would have held—her forty years should have imposed. It is said that when, from time to time, Simon Blum with his pack came strolling down the road from Vicente's adobe, Encarnación could not resist buying some bit of jewelry that especially became her, or a silk shawl. And if she did not have the money on hand to pay for it, as few did in a land where hides and tallow were still the chief currency, what did it matter, since her signature on a bit of paper answered just as well? This doubtless helped hasten the day when ease and plenty were over for the Altamiranos; a sheriff's sale was ordered by the court, and their homestead, with "tenements, hereditaments and appurtenances" was sold at public auction, for $780.

Encarnación had no children—another thing that sets her apart in that period of fecundity—and after her gay times at the Presidio, life in the little valley may have seemed very dull to her. How did the ladies of those early days pass the long intervals between the rodeos and the fiestas, we wonder? They rode horseback, we are told, almost as well as the men. They governed great households and did exquisite needlework. Until queues went out of fashion, they combed and braided the hair of fathers, brothers, and husbands every day. They made bread and candles and soap, or directed those enterprises; and some of them, it is said, were capable of taking charge of the sowing and harvesting of crops. And some, like Guadalupe Vallejo, passionately loved their countrysides. Guadalupe's father, José de Jesús Vallejo, a brother of Mariano, was in charge of the secularized Mission San José. In her old age she wrote this account of washday on a Spanish rancho:

"The night before [the washday expedition] the Indians had soaped the clumsy carreta's great wheels. Lunch was placed in baskets, and the gentle oxen were yoked to the pole. We [children] climbed in, under the green cloth of an old Mexican flag which was used as an awning, and the white-haired Indian *gañan* [teamster], who had driven the carreta since his boyhood, plodded beside with his long *garrocha*, or ox-goad. The great piles of soiled linen were fastened on the backs of horses, led by other servants, while the girls and women who were to do the washing trooped along by the side of the carreta. All in all, it made an imposing cavalcade, though . . . it was generally sunrise before we had fairly reached the spring. The oxen pulled us up the slope of the ravine where it was so steep that we often cried, 'Mother, let us dismount and walk, so as to make it easier.' . . . The watchful mother guided the whole party, seeing that none strayed too far after flowers, or loitered too long talking to the others. Sometimes we heard the howl of coyotes, and the noise of other wild animals in the dim dawn, and then none of the children were allowed to leave the carreta.

"A great dark mountain rose behind the hot spring, and . . . we climbed the cañon to where columns of white steam rose among the oaks, and the precious waters, which were strong with sulphur, were seen flowing over the crusted basin, and falling down a worn rock channel to the brook. . . .

". . . the women put home-made soap on the clothes, dipped them in the spring, and rubbed them on the smooth rocks until they were white as snow. Then they were spread out to dry on the tops of the low bushes . . .

". . . To me, at least, one of the dearest of my childish memories is the family expedition from the great thick-walled adobe, under the olive and fig trees of the Mission, to the *Agua Caliente* in early dawn, and the late return at twilight, when the younger children were all asleep in the slow carreta, and the Indians were singing hymns as they drove the linen-laden horses down the dusky ravines."

One can feel the drowsy summer heat, see the summer-brown hills, smell the tarweed—and the dust. Something of the peace and simplicity and serenity that Guadalupe evokes lingers still about Encarnación's little adobe. Hidden behind wide orchards, overshadowed by great sycamores, it is an eloquent reminder of long-vanished somnolent days that some of us elder Californians love to remember.

5. RANCHO MONTE DEL DIABLO

Salvio Pacheco pastured his cattle in the Ignacio Valley at a very early date: 1828, one record says, though about 1834 is usually given as the time he first put them there. His Monte del Diablo grant, however, was not confirmed by Governor Micheltorena until still another decade had gone by. The name of the grant in no way referred to the mountain we call Diablo: this particular devil's "monte" was a thicket. It is true that Salvio's grant lay virtually in Diablo's shadow, but in Spanish and Mexican times the mountain was known as the Cerro de los Bolbones (or Golgones) and the word "monte" had the meaning "wood" or "thicket."

Salvio was a true Californian, having been born in San Diego in 1793. He arrived in Monterey about 1809, served for a while in the Presidio, and by 1824 was alcalde of the Pueblo of San José. His family remained there until the hostile Indians of the Ignacio Valley had been pacified, an achievement perhaps not unconnected with the smallpox epidemic of 1838, which almost exterminated the neighboring Suisunes and may also have decimated the warlike tribes of the Contra Costa. Don Salvio was wounded by an Indian arrow in one skirmish near the thicket of that devil who not many years later appears to have had his dwelling exorcized, for it became the site of a village named for all the saints. Whether or not Don Salvio attributed his misfortune to this *diablo*, he left his eldest son Fernando, though still a lad, to pitch camp within a mile or so of the meadow where he later built his house, and fight himself into security as best he might.

Although there were rude palizada shelters on the rancho in the middle 'thirties, Don Salvio (sometimes called Don Juan Salvio) did not build his own adobe dwelling and bring his family there until 1847. By that time he was a man of substance, and he built accordingly—a two-storied house, finely proportioned and situated on a rise of ground overlooking the Ignacio Valley. It is still standing in Todos Santos, better known now as the town of Concord, but modern additions have destroyed much of the beauty revealed in early photographs.

Fernando, the eldest of five children, strangely enough was released from his father's custody when he came of age, was given fifteen hundred acres of the grant as a reward for his fighting prowess, and, though he was still a bachelor, was even encouraged to build a house of his own. Salvio, it would seem, was something of a revolutionary. San José officials, during his term of office, regarded him as a public menace. They complained of dangers resulting from his political intrigues, and of the violence of his younger son against foreigners. And at an earlier date he was ordered imprisoned for eight days at Santa Clara because he had used offensive language in a letter to General Vallejo.

One does not readily envisage the Spanish Californian as a Puritan, yet some hint of Puritanism does emerge now and again from the chronicles. It was a holdover, perhaps, from the days of the padres' dominance—witness their denunciations, blithely disregarded for the most part, against the waltz. Another sin, vigorously inveighed against, history would seem to indicate went the same gay and untrammeled way. Young men would stand at a church door and stare at women as they came from mass. The dignity of the church, the morals of the young people, and the community's peace all were menaced by this abominable practice, it would appear. The Californians are often reproached by their conquerors for a lack of initiative, but to us today this church-door indiscretion seems strangely like the first faint whistle of the wolf.

Don Salvio, at any rate, did not disdain innovation. Such scanty records as we have of him credit him with high intelligence and an ability to adapt himself to the changing times. Indeed, he was one of the few Spanish Californians of his day who died wealthy. Perhaps Salvio's ejection of his first-born was rooted in part in practical considerations. What if the beams of the upper floor of his splendid new adobe had threatened to bend under his son's tread? Fernando was California's weightiest citizen—there was between three hundred and fifty and four hundred pounds of him, gossip held. For the incredulous, his photograph should dispel the last doubt. It still hangs on the wall of his adobe, a mile or two from Concord on the road to Avon, opposite that of his wife.

Don Fernando, William E. Colby says, was an immense man, round as an egg. The sight of him made an indelible impression on a child of four or five. It is sometimes said that two chairs were needed for Fernando when he sat down. But George Griffin, who as a boy knew the Spaniard well, says that he used a special chair with a hinged shelf in front, like the tray of a child's high chair, designed to support his paunch. A special surrey, low slung, with a floor that barely cleared the road, allowed him to step easily from it to the ground. On his rancho there was a swimming pool, fed by artesian wells. Don Fernando loved to bathe, though he could not swim. A contraption was rigged up—a chair on a derrick, perhaps not unlike that used some centuries earlier to lift an armed knight onto his horse—and the servants dipped Fernando in and hoisted him out; dip, hoist, dip, hoist, until he was satisfied. Something else, too, had to be designed especially for him—a coffin unprecedently wide and deep and strong.

Don Fernando's little adobe is said to have been a great center of hospitality. A much simpler dwelling than his father's, it had only three small rooms. Fernando married a widow, Figueroa Jures, with one son, and had six children of his own. His adobe had the usual attic space, reached by an outdoor staircase, where customarily the servants or vaqueros slept. Cooking was done in a roofed but unwalled shed in a patio. Ultimately, additional buildings were erected, among them a large wooden structure for a much-needed dining room. For Fernando was a noted epicure, and guests, even to the number of thirty or forty, had a way of drifting in to dinner—uninvited perhaps, yet never unwelcome. Every night a young lamb was consumed. But the feast of feasts was in June, on Saint John's Day, a day of gaiety filled with bullfights, barbecues, horse racing, and dancing, of course.

One hears much of these dances and feasts and rodeos, little of a ranchero's everyday life. That was not wholly devoid of work. A single item mentioned in an account of the activities of Rancho Monte del Diablo cannot have been an easy chore: to round up and shut up for the night—every night—a thousand calves. The Indians had been subdued, but not the grizzly bears. As late as 1864, it is reported, a mother bear and cub were shot only a mile or two outside Oakland; and Diablo's canyons must have kept the threat of them alive in the Ignacio Valley much later. That Fernando's wife, at least, led no life of indolence, the careworn, anxious face in her photograph well attests. And her husband is said to have busied himself with the welfare of the poorer Mexicans on his rancho and in the neighboring village of Pacheco —indeed, to have been a good friend to the whole countryside.

This father and son seem to have won a place in the affection of their American neighbors that few of the rancheros could boast. Their names still bring smiles to the lips of old people, and words of warm friendliness. Yet praise, oddly enough, often turns to laughter, even to burlesque, as if the derision due a fat man must somehow cloak his father too. A reporter from the San Francisco *Call*, telling of an evening spent with Don Salvio in 1868, extols the Spaniard's intelligence and wit, yet records no better instance of it than the old man's observation that an early California governor wore in his sombrero a plume as long as his arm and had a queue as long as a Chinaman's. When Don Salvio presents a banner to the fire department of the town of Pacheco, acknowledgement is lost in a grinning allusion to gold lace. The *Contra Costa Gazette* grumbles that a San Francisco paper, in reporting the death of a Don Francisco Pacheco, has said that "Pachecoville was named after him." This, of course, the *Gazette* says, is a mistake. Salvio Pacheco, the man for whom the town was named, is very much alive: he "looked like anything but a corpse when we saw him in our streets a day or two since." Two weeks later, the *Gazette*'s temper has worn a bit thin. "The *Morning Call* seems determined to extinguish Don Salvio, whether or no. In attempting to correct its former mistake it says, 'Francisco Pacheco, who resides in that vicinity, is not dead, but another Pacheco, Salvio of Monterey, is.' Don Francisco *is* dead. Don Salvio is *not*. Do you sabe now?"

The *Morning Call*, however, reflected little more than the usual confusion. Many stories about early California are alternately asserted and denied and are often impossible to verify. Even the personal recollections of pioneers, too often written years after the events they record, are frequently erroneous in their dates and facts. A narrative about early days in Pacheco village is a case in point. Once a thriving center for teamsters carrying freight between the Santa Clara and San Ramon and Napa valleys, Pacheco was wiped out by floods in the late 'sixties. Merchants suffered enormous losses. As a business center the town had to be abandoned. Thereupon, in 1869, a local chronicle says, Fernando Pacheco and Francisco Galindo offered to lay out another town and give lots to the ruined merchants to enable them to start business again. Descendants of the Pacheco and Galindo families, however, say that it was Salvio, not Fernando, who made the gift, and certain facts bear them out. For it was around the paternal adobe, not near Fernando's house, a mile or two away, that the new village of Todos Santos made its start.

Facts must always claim the major consideration, yet legend helps to tell the story of the brief flowering of a race. Not Spanish, not Mexican, assuredly not American. Physically, the more acute early observers say, the Californians were superior to their progenitors. They were kindly, pious, generous—to offset the sins that foreigners oftenest taxed them with. About those sins José Arnaz has a few illuminating words to say. Before the days when the foreigners began to arrive in considerable numbers, little intoxicating liquor was consumed in California, and there was virtually no drunkenness. Monte was seldom played. "faro was unknown, the social game at cards was *malilla*, something like whist . . . extensively played but not for money. . . . There were so to speak no poor people. If a person wanted meat and had none were not the cattle on a thousand hills his?" The garden of the wealthy man was open to him; olives and grapes and oranges were so abundant that they went to waste. "Helping one's self to a horse or an ox or a sack of fruit was not . . . called stealing. . . . What was the use of quarrelling for a few hundred head of horses or cattle between owners who could not estimate the number belonging to them . . ."

Unhappily, Arnaz goes on to say, there are some who "will not lift a finger for themselves, if lifting it will give them fields and fruits illimitable. Where . . . the rich esteem their riches lightly, part with them easily, what is the use says the lazy vagabond of taking up land, planting . . . having to think for yourself and act for yourself . . . when you have some one to be and to do all this for you . . . One had all one wanted without bothering about it."

Leaving aside a few details concerning Indian abuses, filthy houses, nonexistent education, and the like, which to the modern mind somewhat disturbs this idyllic picture, Don José Arnaz in this account shows that his day oddly parallels certain aspects of our own. Under the paternalism of the great landowners, the rank and file of the population showed an increasing distaste for initiative and steady work. "Let the government agencies do the worrying," we begin to say. Where easy security is in question, perhaps those indolent early Californians had a make-up not altogether unlike our own.

Their way of life is gone, incomprehensible, indeed antagonistic to American mores of today. Yet the thought will recur that perhaps, in the pushing, crowded decades that followed the conquest of California, something might have been gained for Americans if that earliest enjoyment of simple forms of living had not been so quickly and so completely overborne.

Part Two ∾

A SCOT, A POLE, AND TWO AMERICANS

6. THE STONE HOUSE AND JOHN MARSH

The Stone House, standing empty now as it has for many years, has a cold, unfriendly look. It was greatly admired in its day. Before it was quite finished it was described as a "pleasing and appropriate union of manor house and castle," an "architectural gem" that "has departed from the stereotyped square box . . . called a house in California." It departed too, unhappily, from any suggestion of comfort and hospitality. A tight, gloomy structure, barren of any charm, even its site is prosaic, though Mrs. Marsh is said to have selected it herself. She never lived in the Stone House. She died before it was finished, and her husband, "a man of great intelligence, of varied accomplishments, and singular experience of life," was murdered only a few weeks after he had moved into it.

The owner of this house called himself Doctor John Marsh. He held no medical diploma, though he had made some study of medicine. Soon after his arrival in California, the ayuntamiento of the pueblo of Los Angeles had granted him a license to practice medicine. Indeed, at a time when throughout Alta California medical help was virtually unavailable, his qualifications ranked high.

The Stone House is not many miles from Martinez. Toward the end of his life, Dr. Marsh, following approximately Fages' route of 1772 across the hills, could cover the road with horse and surrey in less than a day. But when the huge Rancho Los Meganos ("ranch of the dunes") first became his, in April, 1838, it was a wild, remote, and inaccessible place. Indian raids had been so troublesome that José de la Guerra y Noriega had been glad to sell Marsh his grant. The land stretched from the sandy banks of the San Joaquin River up Marsh Creek to the base of Mount Diablo. The nearest rancheros were Ignacio Martínez, Salvio Pacheco, and Ignacio Sibrian, who later became Marsh's enemy. The only other American on the Contra Costa was Robert Livermore, and the nearest settlement was Mission San José.

Marsh possibly found solitude not unwelcome. By all accounts he was not a neighborly person—"a kind of crank from Harvard College who settled here . . . in an adobe hut and achieved distinction as a misanthrope and miser, sympathetic with the mountain spirit at whose feet he crouched." His moody temperament and penny-saving ways had nothing in common with the carefree openhandedness of the Spanish Californians. Most of them heartily disliked him. Once when he traveled to town with his load of

Fort Ross, Sonoma County

General Vallejo's Adobe, Petaluma

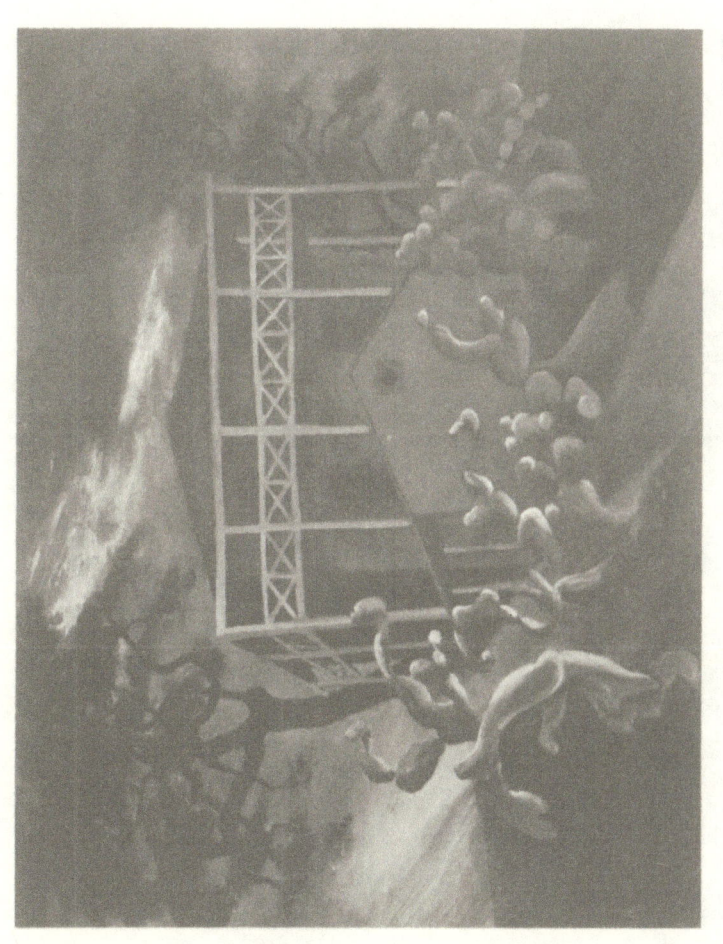

Victor Castro's Adobe, San Pablo

A Martínez Adobe, Alhambra Valley

John Marsh's House, near Byron

John Strentzel's and John Muir's House, near Martinez

Schoolhouse and Graveyard, Columbia

Gravevard. Columbia

Pellaton's Store, Mokelumne Hill

St. Canice Church, Nevada City

Bonanza Kelly's House, near Suscol

Napa Soda Springs, Napa County

Woodward's Gardens, San Francisco

James Flood's "Linden Towers," Menlo Park

Adolph Sutro's House, San Francisco

The Hopkins and Stanford Houses, San Francisco

hides, he was even grudged a bed and had to sleep under his cart. The more cultivated Spaniards acknowledged his fine qualities and attainments in polite phrases wholly lacking in cordiality.

Yet the man who built the Stone House—cold, stingy, unfriendly though his contemporaries may have labeled him—could not have been wholly without generosity and warmth. His Indians, serfs though they undoubtedly were, rated him their friend. He freely dosed their malaria with the precious quinine, doctored them as faithfully as he might have treated a Vallejo child, or a Castro. To these wealthy neighbors his fees ran high. Fifty to a hundred and fifty cows a visit, according to the length of the journey or his reluctance to undertake it. And the journeys were indeed long. His practice covered a large part of central California. A call once came from Vicente Martínez, to attend his wife, Guadalupe Moraga, in Merced; but she died before the Doctor's horse could cover the ninety miles. On another occasion, on a summons from General Vallejo, Dr. Marsh traveled in an open boat the whole length of San Francisco Bay, from the landing near Mission San José to Sonoma.

In this earlier time no thought of an elegant stone mansion entered Dr. Marsh's mind. He lived as his neighbors did in the Ignacio Valley, in the Cañada del Hambre, and in San Ramon. His Indians built him an adobe on Marsh Creek where the foothills debouch into the plain. His cattle ranged widely over his hills, which were infested with thieves from time to time, though cattle stealing was not so frequent in early years as later. He took a squaw for mistress, a circumstance not unusual, though in his case the neighbors made it something of a scandal. He was not altogether a hermit: letters testify to that—letters so informal, even jocular, in their manner as to suggest that the Spanish view of Marsh's character was not altogether shared by the growing group of Americans. Charles Weber in 1846 threatens that if Marsh does not soon write the articles about California which he alone can write, he will send no more newspapers to him, and he "may rot in your stinking soap factory. Bah!" And from the new settlement beyond the Soscol, John Gantt, writing to Marsh in 1847 about the hot springs in Napa, says: "I am at this place for the benefit of my health, having been advised by Doctor Powell to use the warm bath frequently, and can't help thinking myself prematurely fashionable in so doing as it is very mal appropo for poor folks." He then encourages Marsh to come to the valley to find a wife. He recommends two young ladies who are "well worth the ride to see." In fact there are a number of ladies, including "several long built widows . . . in the fertile valley of Nappa."

Marsh did not follow up this suggestion. The companionship of his cherished books continued to temper his lonely existence. He may even have found his solitary life a welcome change from the Indian wars and frontier adventures of the arduous decade which had preceded his coming to California. Even here, however, what with horsethieves, bandits, and Mexican revolutions, adventure was not wanting. Some of it was of his own seeking, his trip to the Yuba gold fields in May, 1848, for instance. He found gold there, but not altogether from the diggings. He became a trader. His cattle, until then worth only some two dollars a head, no longer represented merely hides but became meat for the hungry miners. The dunes along the San Joaquin River, which had given the Rancho los Meganos its name, became a humming embarcadero. John Marsh had become a rich man. Yet he was still living in the original tule-thatched adobe, with dirt floors and unglazed windows, when in 1851 he met Abby Tuck.

She was a Massachusetts girl, attractive, intelligent, accomplished, moreover of an adventurous spirit to suit his; the lure of California, if not of its gold, had led her to join a Baptist missionary party which sailed from New York in June, 1850. Marsh's courtship and brief marriage form one of the happier passages in a far from happy life. The scholar, the man who would lie on the hearth reading by firelight far into the night, could have encountered few women like Abby since he left Harvard in 1823.

For a while after their marriage in 1851 they lived in the adobe—with a few improvements, one hopes, in the matter of floors and windows—but the Doctor soon began to plan a house better suited to his position. It was to be of stone, and more splendid than any other home in California. He even went to the length of employing an architect. Building the house was a long, slow process. The bricks that went into its construction had to be burned on the place, the stone quarried in the hills. Before it was fairly started, the Marshes' daughter Alice was born. Abby was never quite well afterward. In 1855 she died.

After that, the Doctor's troubles began to increase: trouble with squatters, cattle thieves, vaqueros, a feud with Ignacio Sibrian. The one ray of light in this period was his reunion with Charles Marsh, his son by a French-Indian mother. Before John came to California she had died in Prairie du Chien, and for years he had believed that his son, too, was dead. The account of their reunion, as given by William H. Brewer only a few years after the event, reads like a tale from Andersen or Grimm. The wicked fairy had endowed the long-forgotten son with a slightly malformed foot, and it was by that no less than by his name or by his story that the father recognized him.

The Stone House was finished. For a few weeks, father and son lived there together, the older man spending much of his time on top of the tower with a spy glass, searching his lands for cattle thieves. On September 24, 1856, he started to drive to Martinez, en route, it is said, to San Francisco and a new bride. On the way he was murdered by three of his vaqueros —the ringleader a brother-in-law of Sibrian—who believed that Marsh had with him the five thousand dollars in gold that they had seen him receive from a sale of cattle.

Charles was ultimately recognized as one of the Doctor's heirs, and shared equally with Alice in the great inheritance. For a while he and his family lived in the Stone House, but never in the splendor that Marsh had envisaged. Brewer saw it for the second time in the late 'sixties, after Charles Marsh had sold it and moved away. Then "old chairs with rawhide bottoms occupy rooms with marble mantels," he writes; "the fine mansion is surrounded with a most miserable fence, with hogs in the yard, some of the windows broken, and things slovenly in general." It is tidier, but no less forlorn, today.

7. JOHN STRENTZEL AND JOHN MUIR

Sometime in the late 'fifties, the Cañada del Hambre became the Alhambra Valley. Mrs. John Strentzel is credited with the change of name. She did not like the connotation of hunger in her lovely teeming valley, and thought the name Alhambra, with its suggestion of sunny Spain, at once more pleasant and more appropriate. She and her husband were newcomers to the district, having bought their first acres there in 1851.

They were not newcomers to the West, however. John Strentzel had been on the move since 1840, when he had first landed in New Orleans. He was born at Lublin, Poland, in 1813, but after the revolution of 1830 he fled to Hungary. There he studied medicine at the University of Pesth, and incidentally gained considerable knowledge of wine making and vine culture. After coming to America, he practiced medicine near the present town of Dallas, Texas, where in 1843 he married Louisiana Erwin. Frémont's reports drew them early to California. The young couple joined a wagon train of 135 persons, including 9 women and 25 children—a company which had to find its own way for 800 miles. They crossed the Rio Grande on a raft, traversed the Mojave Desert in blinding sandstorms. At San Diego, unable to sell their animals for anything like their value, the Strentzels started north, again by land.

They settled finally on the Tuolumne River, a mile or two below what is now La Grange, put up tents, established a ferry, hotel, and store to accommodate travelers between Mariposa and Stockton. In this and still another venture in the great river valleys their gains were wiped out by floods. With health considerably impaired by their privations, they went to Benicia, where they were fortunate enough to meet a former neighbor from Texas who told them about the Contra Costa.

The privations were not quite over. Their only shelter on the new-bought land was little better than the huts of hide and tules that had housed the earliest Spanish settlers. But that phase did not last long: their first house was completed within the year. A picture of it, a lithograph printed in the late 'seventies, shows a simple and charming story-and-a-half cottage, white-painted, one would suppose, built on much the same lines as the neighboring Altamirano adobe. That cottage is said to exist still, incorporated in the nondescript house of the 'eighties that stands today upon the low rise of ground. It has been remodeled many times, and until quite recently has been occupied continuously by members of the family, down to Dr. Strentzel's great-great-grandchildren.

Bit by bit, Dr. Strentzel bought Alhambra Valley land: twelve acres, "more or less" from the Altamiranos, for which he paid two hundred and fifty dollars; Vicente Martínez' land, and his adobe, which he had sold to a man named Franklin, for whom Franklin Canyon was named; and land from the Las Juntas grant. By 1860 Dr. Strentzel's wonderful peaches had begun to win prizes at county fairs. We read of an exhibit at a racecourse where he and his wife and little daughter Louise share honors with other prize winners: José de Jesús Martínez, for a horse; José's daughter Isabella, best equestrienne (the losing contestants were each awarded a gold thimble); and Guadalupe Martínez, Vicente's daughter, for embroidery. Already, however, the Spanish names have begun to fade on the history pages. Accounts of travelers ignore them, or speak them only with contempt. Even Brewer, in his ramblings up and down the state, seemed hardly aware that Spaniards once owned the land. Yet if he had wanted to be reminded of them, or to realize more sensitively just what the American enterprise that he so lauded really entailed, he had only to glance at certain columns recurring daily in the newspapers—those that advertised the sheriff's sales. One distinguished name after another appeared. Whatever the faults or negligences of the Spanish Californians may have been, one bitter truth cannot be ignored: the rancheros had had no experience at all with money. Hides and tallow and land constituted their wealth. They were the easy dupes of clever traders like Simon Blum, who, within the law, loaned them money on mortgages that were later foreclosed with the inevitability of night following day.

Dr. Strentzel, who himself belonged to a conquered race, had no part in squatters' or usurers' ways of acquiring property. His growing prosperity was based on the same sturdy thrift and perseverance that had carried him through the hardships and losses of his earlier California days, and on his scientific approach to agriculture. Indeed, his scientific reputation was the attraction that in the late 'seventies first brought a young visitor to the ranch.

John Muir's first summer in the California mountains was only six or seven years behind him when he met Louie Strentzel. Tactless friends had been urging upon him acquaintance with this charming girl until he was a bit wary. It was to converse with the Doctor that he came: that must be understood. Converse with the Doctor he did—for a while. Then we hear of an exchange of views on flowers; of a box of ranch grapes that pursued John Muir all over Nevada one October and reached him at last, miraculously fresh because it had been so carefully packed by delicate hands; of a "fascinator" found incomprehensibly in a pocket; of his abomination of San Francisco's crowded dwellings; and so, eventually, of a wedding.

On a hilltop overlooking the lower end of his vineyards, Dr. Strentzel then built the big square house with the towering cupola that is now known as John Muir's house. The young couple went on living in the little cottage farther up the valley, rejoicing in improvements always dear to John Muir's heart—added window space and an open fireplace. After the Doctor's death in 1890, John and Louie, with their little daughters Wanda and Helen, went to live in the new mansion with Mrs. Strentzel. It became their permanent home. The children grew up there, and Mr. Muir lived in this house until his death in 1914.

The place has a dual personality, as indeed its more famous master had. The once handsome house is stiff, practical, more than a little dour, reflecting that cool, almost "near" Scotch business sense that John Muir's harried overseer knew all too well. "Could you not have done with less?" the master of the ranch, newly returned from his magic mountains, would demand. And the overseer, hard put to it to finance the long summer months with the inflexible amount accorded him, would mutter that indeed the ranch *should* have done with quite a lot more. Yet it prospered and made money for a man who would have been neither farmer nor businessman had the choice been freely his.

It was in the garden, in those days, that the other man—the poet, the idealist—could best be found. One still finds a trace of him in some exotic plant half smothered in weeds, or in a beloved tree, grown now out of all his recognition, that he had planted and tended. As for the house, it was a cold, empty, echoing place when I knew it best, in the year before John Muir's death. Mrs. Muir had died several years before, and the daughters were both married. Wanda, Mrs. Thomas Hanna, at the time was living in Vicente Martínez' old adobe, a five-minute walk from the big house. Mr. Muir used to go there for his meals, whenever he could be beguiled from his favorite refreshments, fruit and cheese and French bread. He occupied the mansion alone, though a legendary Chinaman lived somewhere on the premises—at least he was said to materialize now and again to clean Mr. Muir's study, though I never saw any evidence either of him or of the cleaning.

I was spending a day or two every week on the ranch that summer, helping Mr. Muir with some typewriting. His work on *Travels in Alaska* had been going badly. A highly skilled stenographer who resented having to sit with folded hands while he discoursed at length about his adventures had driven him to distraction. To have no interest in glaciers, and to prefer getting the day's work done to listening to a monologue—a conversation, Mr. Muir called it—to its furthest end was not only a mark of sin but also of a complete lack of intelligence. What I lacked in competence as a secretary was happily offset by my love of mountains and my willingness to let him talk of them. Those long evenings, especially, spent by his fireside, bring back to me my clearest picture of his fine-featured, spirited face, alight with the recollections of what he once called his "bully life."

His study, the upper room in the corner to the right of the front door, was the heart of the house. It was a den of books—and dust—with a little oasis of comfort and cheer in front of the open fireplace. Easy chairs stood there, and the cluttered writing table. Above the fireplace, instead of the vast mirror that the period exacted, hung an equally vast painting by William Keith, a dark painting—of oaks, as I remember it. It, too, was dimmed by dust; and inserted in its frame and lined up along the marble mantel were photographs of John Muir's friends. When, in moments of fireside ease, he spoke of someone, he would rise and take the picture in hand, run a finger over the surface until the features emerged, and then set it back again. The record of these friendly ruminations would stand there, untouched, week after week until the clean face was masked in dust again.

8. JOHN BIDWELL'S HOUSE

My painting was not right at all, my visitor told me. I had put the accent on the cupola—painted a mansion. The important part of the house, actually, was behind a certain window under the porch, where the General sat with his books. A few days later, however, a letter assured me that the writer had approved the feeling of the picture, even though no one's best effort of imagination could equal "the picture of grandeur and happiness that surmounts that building in my mind."

"I would expect," Dr. Graham further wrote, "to see a big man . . . carving a great big cassava, and a pretty petite wife looking on with admiration; . . . many books, far more than any human being could ever read; and fine long banisters that any boy would like to slide down, ending in a broad porch running nearly around the house for boys to play tag on. There should be a large four-seated carryall holding at least sixteen boys and Peter driving the finest two horses in California, the back of the "carriage" containing enough goodies for everybody and more to come. There must be two bridges and a flour mill across from the wagon bridge . . . an apricot tree at one side of the house if not an orchard with boys climbing into every tree. If you get tired of painting in front, go to the back, put in the Indian woman waiting for a hand-out, with Mrs. Bidwell saying a prayer for her before she gets the grub. In case you put in a rose bush, be sure and get the aphis on the roses, else the General will have nothing to talk about save the latin name of the rose and where it originated. The aphis has a name, too, so label it."

If to Dr. Graham the memory of John Bidwell's home is a picture of happiness and generosity and simple, kindly living, other witnesses have it that the element of grandeur was not wholly lacking. In the prodigal extravagance of the California of Bidwell's latter days, a man of his eminence could hardly escape some touch of baronial splendor. For though he was one of the earliest American settlers, his long life spanned pioneer conditions, gold-rush days, bonanza frenzies, and reached into the period of industrial expansion and agricultural development and the dominance of railway kings.

Bidwell had arrived in California before the gold rush. As early as 1840, when he was only twenty-one, a letter written by John Marsh had turned his thoughts toward California. The next year, with some sixty others, he had joined the first wagon train that crossed the plains and mountains to California. Of the many accounts of that journey, Bancroft's "The travellers . . . met with no disasters except the accidental death of one man—and two marriages" is the most succinct. Bidwell's own journal, with its hint of a crow and wild-cat diet, suggests that disaster may have been imminent.

At the end of their long journey, in November, 1841, the pilgrims stopped for a few days at Los Meganos. But John Marsh, though he had promoted immigration, did not particularly relish entertaining so large and hungry a group of immigrants. Bidwell thought him stingy and inhospitable—tricky, moreover, for he cannily cut food losses by charging his guests for government passports, which Bidwell subsequently found were issued free.

Later that same month Bidwell and his party moved on to Sutter's Fort. Early the next year he was sent to Fort Ross to superintend the removal of the cattle and equipment that Sutter had bought from the Russians when they abandoned their settlement. Included in this equipment was a quantity of old French flintlock muskets which Sutter thought had probably been lost by Bonaparte's army in the retreat from Moscow. From time to time, in the California story, one comes across some such unexpected link with European history: Salvador Vallejo, for instance, found that an old Spaniard engaged to repair the mission church at Sonoma had been a carpenter aboard the battleship *Santissima Trinidad* at the Battle of Trafalgar.

This Ross assignment was to lead to Bidwell's acquisition of his great Rancho Chico. On his return to Sutter's Fort, when he camped for the night at the rancho of Manuel Vaca, some of his horses were stolen by an Oregon-bound party camped in the vicinity. After making his report to Captain Sutter, Bidwell followed them northward and ultimately overtook the travelers and recovered his horses. In the process of pursuing the horsethieves he explored on horseback most of the upper Sacramento Valley, and, on the site of the present town of Chico, found the Mecca of his long journey—the land that eventually he bought. From his observations on that hasty covering of the great valley, Bidwell drew a map that was adopted by the Mexican government and used as evidence of landownership long after the American conquest.

Rumors of the existence of gold in California—aside from the unprofitable traces found in the south—had come early to Bidwell's attention. In the spring of 1844, Pablo Gutiérrez told him that there was gold in the Sierra Nevada and said that if he had a *batea* (wooden bowl) he could prove it. Bidwell, thinking that some complicated machinery was needed, asked where Pablo could get a *batea*. Down in Mexico, was the reply; and Bidwell in all innocence offered to pay Pablo's expenses if he would go and fetch one. But, fortunately for Bidwell's pocketbook, the Castro-Alvarado insurrection against Micheltorena delayed this enterprise, and in the uprising, Pablo Gutiérrez lost his life.

During the Mexican War, Bidwell was placed by Frémont in charge of Mission San Luis Rey, to inventory the mission property and protect the Indians still living there. On his return from war service, his great ranch of twenty-six thousand acres along the Sacramento River became his chief concern. He made a horseback journey of twelve hundred miles to secure cuttings of fruit trees and vines from Mission San Luis Rey; and by 1849, in spite of the distraction of the discovery of gold at Bidwell's Bar, his was one of the most promising ranches in California.

A log cabin was his first habitation, and then in 1852 he built the adobe ranch house in which he lived until his marriage to Annie Kennedy in 1868. For her he built the big wide-verandaed house which (in spite of Dr. Graham's disclaimer) was early called "the Mansion," and was widely known for its generous hospitality. The guest might be General Sherman, Joseph Le Conte, President Hayes, or, less welcome, Leland Stanford, who once came with a horde of unexpected luncheon guests, anxious to make it appear that Bidwell supported the railroad magnate in his political ambitions. And starred among these more formal visitors was John Muir, who with Asa Gray and Sir Joseph Hooker guided the Bidwells on a botanizing expedition to Lassen Peak and Mount Shasta. In Bidwell's friendship with Muir, as well as in his acrimonious encounters with Marsh, one is reminded of how closely interrelated all these widely spaced early landowners really were. On horseback, in carretas, by stagecoach, railway, or riverboat—as well as in automobiles on freeways—Californians seem always to have been on the move.

Today, the old mansion, separated from Chico's busy streets only by its grove of gigantic trees, has a dreamy, somnolent quality far different from the hivelike activity of its earlier years. John Bidwell's acres produced wheat, fruit, raisins, and vegetables. Agriculture, irrigation, transportation, education, even politics engaged his active interest. His wife busied herself with the welfare of the Indians on their estate. She taught them reading and household arts, built a chapel for them, and was ordained as its regular pastor. Her work for the National Indian Association and for temperance and woman suffrage continued long after the General's death in 1900.

"Precious" was his chosen name for her; but she, with the formality of wives of her period, always addressed him as "General." A gracious, warmhearted, generous couple, the best of their generation, it is pleasant to think of them as Dr. Graham does, as reveling in the swarm of neighbor children sliding down the banisters and climbing the orchard trees.

Part Three

THE FORTY-NINERS TURN RESPECTABLE

9. A GRAVEYARD AND A SCHOOL

The story of California's rowdy population—the bandits, the cutthroats, the Chileans, the Sydney ducks—has been told over and over again, to the neglect of other elements. It comes somewhat as a surprise, therefore, to find that two of the oldest surviving buildings in two of the early and once most populous diggings are a little brick schoolhouse and a little parish church. Whether the communities owed these to the men's talent for self-government which Charles Shinn so extols, or to the civilizing influence of the women who increasingly "graced this rough part of creation with their presence," remains a matter of conjecture.

From many an early diary or manuscript of pioneer "recollections" one gathers evidence that the California of gold-rush days was preëminently a man's world. There were women in the wagon trains that crossed the plains, of course, and children too; but with few exceptions, such as the Dame Shirley letters, neither their stories nor their impressions have been given prominence. Bayard Taylor, at Sacramento in the late fall of 1849, does note that the women who had come overland seemed "to have stood the hardships of the journey remarkably well, and were not half so loud as the men in their complaints." But he gives even more space to the appearance of the emigrant cattle. "The beasts," he says, "had an expression of patient experience which plainly showed that no roads yet to be traveled would astonish them in the least. . . . Much toil and suffering had given to their countenances a look of almost human wisdom." The cows, he admits before passing on to his brief comment on womankind, "had been yoked in with the oxen and made to do equal duty."

The 'fifties, however, were to bring changes. Women all over the western world had begun to rebel against their long subjection. In Europe, Hannah More's *Strictures on the Modern System of Female Education*, Mary Wollstonecraft's *Vindication of the Rights of Women*, and the growing reputation (whether good or ill) of Harriet Martineau and George Sand; at home, the activities of Lucretia Mott, Elizabeth Cady Stanton, and Susan B. Anthony, to say nothing of Amelia Jenks Bloomer—all had had their cumulative effect in goading women to a new sense of their "rights." Moreover, the women who braved the hardships of a journey to California, either by land or by sea, were not the least enterprising and able of their generation. Abby Tuck, for example, or another indomitable woman—known to me in her old age—who, when her place in a wagon train was usurped by a man who might be more useful on the journey, bought a team of horses and a wagon and triumphantly drove herself and her infant daughter across the plains.

Newspapers soon begin to reflect the new order. From an eastern source a San Francisco journal quotes the advertisement: "This is to give notice that John Henry Coville, has left his bed and board somewhere in the middle of December, 1846, and if he gives no information where he can be found from within three months, I shall get married again, and leave the city. Elizabeth Coville." Again, a growing sense of a divorce-crisis brings stern reproof to Alcalde Boggs of Sonoma. Doesn't he know that he had no business to divorce Isaac Flint and Sarah Flint? He cannot divorce Catholics, because only the Church can do that, or Protestants, because California has no law as yet about divorce. What every man can and should do is intimated over and over again in this and succeeding decades: help discourage this goldarned business of giving strong-minded women their heads. The bloomer costume and woman's unwomanly hankering after an education come in for their share of denunciation. As for those supremely unfeminine creatures who actually venture to travel alone on steamers or stagecoaches, someone should invent an artificial baby for their protection—a bundle with a squeal inside, to ward off any predatory male who might attempt to sit beside the lone lady and thus offend her delicacy.

Perhaps there really was some need of labeling an

irreproachable and unapproachable lady while on her travels, for the rapidly growing population of California soon included young women no less enterprising than Abby Tuck, if not quite so respectable. The ship *Iconium* from Boston was reported to have arrived in San Francisco with a cargo of thirty-five unmarried young females, and another shipment was said to be on the way. Women in San Francisco, Daniel Lévy maintains, with a few most honorable exceptions, belong to the "demi monde et quart de monde" —the nadir, one gathers, of the disreputable. And at the surprisingly good restaurants, though served by "complaisantes" young Hebes, the clients unhappily too often find themselves "aussi plumés que rassasiés" when they leave.

What the chroniclers of the hell-roaring period usually fail to mention is the comparatively short time during which lawlessness held complete sway. In Columbia a lynching did occur as late as 1858, but as an exceptional occurrence; the place had long been a well-ordered community. Even in those most chaotic months between the close of the Mexican War and the formulation of a state constitution, many individual citizens emerged who were strong enough and wise enough to begin to shape a tolerable community life long before any legal endorsement of it existed. The forty-niner "often appears in literature as a dialect-speaking rowdy, savagely picturesque, rudely turbulent; in reality, he was a plain American citizen cut loose from authority, . . . forced to make the defence and organization of society a part of his daily business. In its best estate, the mining-camp of California was a manifestation of the inherent capacity of the race for self-government."

In support of the theory that women had their share in defending and organizing this new society, we find Hildreth's Diggings (as Columbia was originally called) early putting itself on record in doing homage to the fair sex. When it was rumored that the first real lady was coming to town, the miners all quit work and marched four miles down the trail, with a band, to meet her. From far in the mountains the miners came, just to get a glimpse of a phenomenon elsewhere nostalgically described as a "dear bewitching creature." One hopes that the lady proved worthy of the sacrifice of the day's gold, that she was attractive, yet not glamorous enough to arouse her husband to the frenzy of jealousy that Frank Marryat describes in another spouse. Some miners had stared at his pretty wife while they breakfasted, which made him so furious that "his skin cracked." But he insisted that he was a "devilish good fellow" when he was "right side up." Evidently the wrong side remained uppermost all day, for the wife at suppertime still looked as if she expected any moment to be her last.

This feted lady was apparently not the first woman in the diggings: she was said to have been the first "good one." The good ones were treated with unfailing civility—except by the bad ones. Big Anne, one of the worst, had, it was reported, grievously insulted one of the best. It was decided that Big Anne had to be rebuked. The fire department turned out en masse. They ran their fire engine, "Papeete," down to Big Anne's shack and hosed her out of bed into the street.

Columbia's little red schoolhouse, high on a hill above the main street, is designated on picture post cards as the first school in Tuolumne County. If local newspapers of the period are to be believed, this is an error. When the building was dedicated with an imposing Masonic ceremony in November, 1860, the neighboring town of Sonora already boasted a public school. Columbia's very first school seems to have been a small Catholic institution, organized soon after the first disastrous fire and before the completion of the historic Saint Anne's Church. For the Protestant children in town, a Mrs. Haley opened a small private school as early as 1853.

Just how public the little school really was remains in some doubt, for "respectable" parents were at first loud in their denunciations of a system that might expose their nice-mannered sons and daughters to the dubious manners and mores of the riffraff offspring of Mexicans and Chileans and Frenchmen and shanty Irish. The school board was shocked. No such children were allowed to enter *their* school. For the sake of the riffraff, one hopes that Saint Anne was less genteel.

The ninety-four females (respectable) that the census of Columbia showed along about 1854 were undoubtedly beginning to have an influence. The patronage of saloons, it was hopefully stated, showed a sharp decline. Social life was taking shape. There were numerous balls, sponsored by the fire company, at which "lovely woman graced the occasion with her approving smiles." A traveling circus came to town. A Vocal Music Society came into being, along with the Columbia Lyceum, devoted to the discussion of living issues of the day. Columbia's theatre was crowded to the doors when the Chapmans played, and perhaps the audience overflowed into the street when the occasion was a "Chaste, Patriotic, Pathetic, Literary, Musical, Humorous Entertainment."

For less professional forms of entertainment the town could always rely on the antics of some local character, such as Pat Shine, the Hydraulic King. Pat's business, it is true, was more aggravation than entertainment to his fellow citizens. He could not forget that his home town was built on land that had once been a part of the richest diggings along the Mother Lode. Whenever he heard that a family was about to move away from Columbia, Pat would make haste to buy their land. Once it was his, the hydraulic hose came into play. A lot on Main Street fared no better than a remote cabin. The house was hosed out of existence and the land bared to its bones in no time. Pat's name was anathema to his neighbors, until the wonderful day when he quarreled with Mike, who kept a saloon. The matter had not proceeded beyond shouting, when Dutch Pete came driving by with a load of melons. Pat bought the entire load—and began to shy fruit at Mike's head. Mike responded with beer mugs, and the battle was on. One infers that Pat was the victor, for the affray is called the Battle of the Melons to this day.

In spite of these alleviations, however, and of the growth of lyceum culture, life still was far from easy. Communications remained slow and difficult. To substitute an ox team for the sluggish U. S. Mail system some critics held might improve matters. Flooding rivers had a way of washing out bridges. Wagon roads in the winter became impassable. Famine threatened the town. Twenty to thirty days it took the freight wagons to get from Stockton to Columbia. And there was a smallpox epidemic. The cemetery filled rapidly that year.

No story of Columbia's cultural development should fail to include the graveyard. It too stands high upon a hill—the same hill, crowding close to the little red schoolhouse, a juxtaposition that runs a bit counter to the best thought on child education today. But to judge by the tombstones in any pioneer cemetery, the cradle and the grave in those times had an association close enough and frequent enough to make the joint site grimly appropriate. Infants of a year and under, young men not yet twenty-five—these, almost without exception, people the earlier graves. A pioneer child of school age must have known quite a lot about death. It was about life that the mothers of a century ago strove to keep their children—their daughters more particularly—ignorant. One wonders what the neuroses of a century hence will find to feed on. Only eternity seems left. And this brings us, with a brief digression to Mokelumne Hill, to our church.

10. CHEZ PELLATON

The little house behind the big hotel had a knowing, indeed a wicked, look. The thick adobe walls of its lower story had been plastered and then painted red. The many-paned glass door, set rakishly askew, the ramshackle wooden balcony, the tumble-down porch roof of weathered shakes sloping down from a rickety balustrade, the close-shuttered windows of the upper story—all contributed to the picture that instantly formed in my mind.

"Mokelumne's hot spot!" I said to myself, entranced. At last I had come upon a true relic of the forty-niners—a dance hall. And in a town of prevailingly French atmosphere at that! I was far too taken with the concept of a cancan graft upon the sturdy limb of native Mother Lode depravity to think then of trying to assemble a few facts. And when I did try, several years afterward, the little house was gone.

Most of its history is gone, too, unhappily. A few people do remember the building, not as a dance hall

—it never was that—but as a store. Antoine Pellaton built it, back in 1852, after he had wearied of the heavy work at the diggings. His stock is said to have been mining equipment, in the beginning; but all that the old people of Pellaton's neighborhood can now remember having bought at his store is candies and tobacco and the little notions carried by a petty business that is fast going downhill—a business clung to long after any profit has been derived from it. How dearly the old Pellatons must have loved their picturesque little shop can be surmised from the pollarded trees that once surrounded it—trees pruned and tended like those in the market square of their native village in France.

Mokelumne Hill has the name of having been one of the wildest of the early mining camps; it had seventeen murders in one week, Daniel Lévy with rather ghoulish relish claims. Bancroft, on the other hand, credits its Vigilance Committee with an earnest attempt to establish legal processes of administering justice "after having from an imperative sense of duty executed one criminal." The first traces of gold were discovered there by some of Stevenson's soldiers in 1848, but the real find was made by a Frenchman while he was fishing for a frog. A nugget worth more than two thousand dollars was his catch for the day. Syrec's Trading Post, the place was first named. Lévy calls it Les Fourcades, after the Fourcade brothers who were early settlers there, and asserts that it was in the main a French settlement.

In Paris, indeed in all France, the gold discovery in California had caused great excitement. Commerce and industry were paralyzed at the moment, owing to successive political disturbances and changes of regime. Many government officials had been thrown out of work. Companies were organized to pay the expenses of some groups, apparently on a commission basis. The first of these arrived in San Francisco as early as September, 1849. One group, under the patronage of the French government and known as the Gardes Mobiles, was made up of former officers and soldiers who had belonged to the corps of that name. Tools and an ample outfit had been supplied for each member and travel expenses had all been provided. Five days after their landing, eighty-two of these Gardes departed for Mokelumne Hill, "maintaining a military appearance which aroused the distrust of the Americans but which was in reality wholly innocent." The thousands of Frenchmen who followed these first gold diggers have been commemorated by many a place name: French Corral, French Flat, French Bar, for instance, though the earliest of all, French Camp, owes its name to French-Canadian trappers who long preceded the gold rush.

Among the Spanish Americans, the French were always popular. Temperamentally they were more akin to the easygoing Spaniards and Mexicans than to the rather grimly industrious Americans. Indeed, misunderstandings between the two antagonistic races became frequent enough in the mining camps to be dignified by the name "the Great French War." The foreign miners' tax, at one time twenty dollars a month, was the main cause of friction; but a fracas might occur without any very understandable excuse.

A Frenchman called Le Vendéen was the butt of much ridicule because he persisted in mining on top of a hill when everyone else was digging away in the canyon bottom. When he made a very rich strike on his hilltop he rashly boasted of his find. An Irishman took offense at this and attacked Le Vendéen. Frenchmen flocked to one side, Irish to the other, and a general melee ensued. The final adjustment, however, was most amicable. It was all a mistake, Le Vendéen explained. The fisticuff manner of settling disputes, man to man, was foreign to the French character. But one could see that, when another Frenchman rushed to one's defense, another Irishman must in honor intervene. And a third Frenchman called for a third Irishman, the Irish gloomily agreed. But they were dead sorry it was *Frenchmen* they had to attack. One can imagine that Lafayette was invoked, and gallant Irish soldiers who had been in exile with James the Pretender. Lévy devotes many paragraphs to the abundant oratory and final peace.

In the little museum in San Andreas, Parisian interest in the diggings is demonstrated by the gold-rush designs on a set of plates, "brought to Mokelumne Hill in early days by Madame Marguerite Mochon," the label says. One plate, inscribed (in French) "A review of troops in the garrison of San Francisco," shows an empty parade ground, with all the soldiers scuttling off for the gold fields. On another, two bearded miners face a still more ferociously bearded bandit. "Aprés avoir découvert une bonne mine," the untranslatable pun reads, "on en rencontre parfois d'assez mauvaise." I myself have a print from a Paris newspaper of the 'fifties: a cartoon by Daumier of two old crones discussing the demand for beautiful women in California and the advisability of departing forthwith to that promising country. That legendary California still lived in the minds of the French on the Pyrenees border when I worked there in 1918. "So you come from California!" more than one peasant of the Landes said to me. "A beautiful country, with much gold."

French Canadians trapped beaver on the Mokelumne River more than a decade before Stevenson's soldiers set foot there; and in mining days a French priest, Father Bobard, visited the district, though Mokelumne had no resident priest. A fair sprinkling of Gaelic citizens must also have been included in the settlement, one surmises, for it boasted a traditional monster that rivaled that of Loch Ness. Several instances of this apparition were reported in the newspapers, although, Richard Coke Wood suggests, the reports came usually at a dull time when there was little else stirring in town. Mr. Peek, it was said, while driving up the hill from the Gwin Mine, heard a scratching sound which he took to be the screech of brakes on a descending wagon. He waited at a turn, but hearing nothing further, started to drive on. Something moving in the chaparral caught his eye—a section of an enormous serpent! His horses took fright and demanded all his attention, so he really didn't see the beast very clearly, he confessed. But he heard it all right—a horrible sound between a hiss and a screech.

However, the name in early Mokelumne Hill history that is best known today is neither French nor Gaelic but Alsatian: Leger, the name of the man who kept the inn on the main street. To a traveler in the year 1859, the establishment seemed to be half German beer hall and half French restuarant. A dance floor was one of its attractions. I entered the hotel barroom, that spring of 1951, to see if I could get a story about old Pellaton's store. The big, dark room stood empty, apparently. As my eyes were adjusting to the gloom after the brilliant sunshine outdoors, a voice said, "Well?"

I jumped. The sound came, I thought, from the long, polished, perfectly empty bar. Ghost stories and monster stories flashed horridly to mind as my eyes caught sight of a bald man's head, laid, it seemed, like John the Baptist's, platter-wise on the near corner of the bar. But it was only the barkeeper, reposing himself on a low stool after the stress of the noon hour. No, he didn't know nothing about the Pellatons. Just that they'd once kept a store. And it hadn't burned down, as I had supposed—just given up and *laid* down from old age. But Mr. Peek, now, over to the courthouse in San Andreas, he'd know all about the Pellatons. But Mr. Peek—not he of Calaveras monster fame—didn't, I found. He said, with truth, that I was a bit late in my pioneer research and passed me on to someone else, who referred me to Daniel Lévy, and to a lady who had gone to Los Angeles. And so I am still looking for someone whose grandmother knew the Pellatons and why they built a shop with a dance-hall connotation and a wicked, secretive look.

11. A PARISH CHURCH

༄ He is not one of the better-known saints, the good man who gave his name to the old church on Nevada City's Coyote Street. He was born in Ireland a very long time ago—about the year 515. His father is said to have been a bard; his mother was named Maul. His early years were spent watching his chieftain's flocks. Under the teaching of several other now little-known saints he became a man of great learning, made a pilgrimage to Rome, and in 565 went to Scotland, where he is known as St. Kenneth. Tradition has it that he founded a monastery at Kilkenny and built the first church at St. Andrew's. The town of Kilkenny commemorates him. And that, perhaps—unless it was because he had more than a hint of the vagabond about him—is the reason why a church in a remote Wild West mining camp was given his name. For two of its earliest priests were Kilkenny born.

The church, however, was not at first called St.

Canice. In the spring of 1853 a little frame building on the same site was dedicated to St. Peter and St. Paul. It burned down a year or two later, and by the time the present brick structure was finished, in the early 'sixties, Nevada City had lost prestige and Grass Valley was preëminent. Father Dalton made his center in the larger town, and Father Griffin, his assistant, named the little brick Church in Nevada City after a cathedral in his birthplace.

These priests, however, were not the founders of the parish. First pioneering honors must go to Father Shanahan, also from Kilkenny, who was nearly sixty years old when he undertook the grinding work of a parish that extended from Downieville to Michigan Bluff—which is to say that it covered the whole upper watershed of the three forks of the Yuba River and a large section of the watersheds of the North and Middle forks of the American. On horseback or muleback he traveled the trails, winter or summer, day or night. Three weeks, it took, merely to cover the miles, up the high ridges, down into the rugged canyons— in fair weather. In winter the higher trails were often blocked with snow, and unending mud clogged them everywhere. The remote, solitary cabins where he visited some of his parishioners boasted none of the luxuries noted several years earlier by Bayard Taylor in the larger mining camps along the Mother Lode. Father Shanahan's parishioners lived in cabins without windows, furnished only with a rough table, a stool, and a bunk. A potato was an almost unknown luxury, though since it was held to be a cure for scurvy it might well have been regarded as a necessity. Salt pork and pancakes were the stand-bys, reinforced occasionally by game when a miner could be persuaded to take time off to hunt. In the heavy winter of 1852–53 conditions in the more inaccessible camps were quite desperate. Flooding rains had brought even Nevada City to the verge of starvation.

It is said of the old priest that he never failed to answer a call or to undertake an arduous journey on the mere suspicion of a need for his services. No matter how many hours he had spent in the saddle that day, if a call came he would put on his boots and start out again. His most exacting test of a young priest was his readiness to accept hardship without a murmur. Small wonder that after Father Shanahan had endured two or three years of this toil and privation, Archbishop Alemany, shocked by the old man's frail appearance, ordered him back to San Francisco and a life of relative ease.

Still another Kilkenny man has a place in Mother Lode history—Patrick Manogue, a miner in Moore's Flat who assisted Father Shanahan at mass there, and later, with the help of the old Father, himself became a priest. For the rest of his life he devoted himself to the miners of the Sierra Nevada and Virginia City. The names of these two priests, and that of Father Dalton, deserve to be enshrined along with those of the early Spanish padres who rode or tramped the mission trails.

To wander about the steep streets of Nevada City today is to be impressed by the number of charming old houses of the 'sixties and 'seventies that are still lived in and still cherished, their paint fresh, their gardens well tended. The old white-toothed brick "castle" on a hilltop is the most arresting, if not the best-kept of these; and its dramatic aspect sets the scene appropriately enough for an old mining town. But the camp first known as Caldwell's Upper Store, and then as the Deer Creek Diggings, and finally, more grandiosely, as Nevada City, today bears few signs of its rowdy beginnings.

In its youthful days, the camp, like its prevailingly young inhabitants, seems to have had a tendency to be a little too big for its boots. It incorporated itself on so grand a scale and with such munificent salaries for its many officials that a year or two later it had to be disincorporated and reorganized on a more frugal basis. It had its due share of disastrous fires. And the usual tall tales are told of its gamblers and "sporting ladies" and bandits. One tale, however, is far from the typical.

Its hero was named Alexander Hunt. He was a printer by trade, and a good one, who worked for many years in the shops of Nevada City's newspapers. He didn't drink—at least he didn't drink too much, or too often. But when on occasion he did indulge himself a little, his chronic obsession would get out of bounds; this was coffins. He slept in one habitually, and home to him was wherever some householder could be persuaded to let him deposit his coffin. Whenever he took a day off and got a little high, he would engage four pallbearers to parade him and his coffin through the streets in funeral procession. Sometimes he would lie down inside "with becoming gravity," but again he would sit upright and gaze abroad, to the mirth or hysterics of the spectators. And one banner night he found a hearse that had carelessly been left outside its rightful habitat. He dragged his coffin to it and deposited it and himself inside. He was still blissfully slumbering there when discovered by passers-by in the morning.

Nevada City had its ups and downs. The first mad rush of miners, the period of pack-train traffic and calico housing, when even in a hotel the traveler might awaken of a stormy morning to find his room afloat and his "shoes chasing one another like boats in a regatta," and when devastating fires were frequent, did not last long. Succeeding it came the era of the great freight wagons with their sixteen-mule teams and their heroic teamsters, less well known to history than their stagecoach brethren, but worthy of a place there, Charles Shinn maintained. The town prospered in the freight-wagon time. Brick buildings replaced the wooden shacks and the tents. Refinement began to radiate from San Francisco, where a group of ladies were publishing a journal of their own, dedicated to Literature and Art. Mrs. Grundy—or should one now say the late Mrs. Grundy?—was frequently invoked in the columns of the *Hesperian*. The weekly was edited by ladies and was written for the most part by ladies. Sometimes it offered original articles—never demoralizing in tone, the editor austerely states—but it oftener depended on reprints from the *Ladies' Repository*. One of these, "The Burden of Dress," has a somewhat startling beginning: "We are all daughters of Eve and all inherit the fig-leaves of her disgrace." However, as we read on, we are reassured. This is merely the author's rather roundabout way of scolding women for thinking too much about the cut of their clothes.

Perhaps the women along the Mother Lode would have been glad of the chance to give a little more time to the frills and flowers and feathers that the lady author so deplored, for hard times came. Many people moved away. The pace of the little towns grew sluggish. Business fell off. The newspapers were reduced to chronicling Fourth of July celebrations with their Grand Parade of Horribles, their sack races, three-legged races, fireworks. There was a ball in North San Juan attended by ladies in silks, crepe shawls, and ribbons; the new floor was so slippery that more than one swain slid across it on his knees and deposited himself thus at his lady's feet. Columns are given over to a discussion of waterfalls—not those of nature's contriving, but those that adorn ladies' heads. In New York, one authority affirms, pumpkin-size waterfalls are *not* good form. The paucity of news reminds one of that depth of inanition reached by a diarist in another community, who wrote, "Did nothing of consequence all day and saw about the same."

Nevertheless, Nevada City never was reduced to the dreariness of many another half-abandoned settlement along the Mother Lode. On the contrary, it experienced a certain revival of business activity before the completion of the transcontinental railroad. For Nevada City offered relatively easy access to the Comstock Lode. From the neighboring settlement of North Bloomfield, a trail—and after 1859 a wagon road—led across Henness Pass and down the Little Truckee River to the Nevada plains. Travel over this pass never rivaled the frantic press, described by J. Ross Brown, on the Placerville route, which was shorter and more readily accessible from the populous areas around Stockton and Sacramento. From Marysville or Grass Valley, however, Henness Pass was the shortest way across the range.

Nevada City was connected in still another way with the development of Virginia City: one of its citizens made the first assay of the baffling and clogging blue dirt which had so annoyed gold diggers on Mount Davidson. An attempt was made to keep the silver discovery secret, but the news soon leaked out and the rush began. Our community lost many of its most enterprising citizens, but there remained a nucleus of conservative businessmen content to build modest fortunes on the needs of miners. Its own mines remained productive, though on a less spectacular scale than in the rival Grass Valley, four miles away. Nevada City is still second in importance to that town, in a businessman's eyes, as it was when Father Dalton relegated the little brick church to a subordinate. To the traveler, however, it stands first, a peaceful and charming little town grown old in grace and dignity.

12. BONANZA KELLY'S RANCH HOUSE

On land once part of the Soscol grant, halfway between Soscol House and the suburbs of Vallejo, there stands an old brick house that today looks like the ghost of its era—an era vanished as irrecoverably as the earlier times of the Indian rancherias and the Spanish ranchos. In a time of growing prosperity between the two frenzies, the gold rush and the bonanza silver excitement, a pioneer agriculturist named Lankershim and his partner bought a ranch of many hundred acres and built a substantial house. Salt-water bricks, it is said, went into its construction; present-day members of the family who used to live in it say that the house is intolerably damp. For that or other reasons it has long stood untenanted. Its wide verandas have rotted and fallen down. The formal gardens, the circular beds of flowers, the fountain—with a pair of bronze children under a dripping bronze umbrella—and the neat gravel walks have all disappeared. The beautiful avenue of cypress trees leading to the front door has been chopped and burned and tortured almost out of existence. Yet the place once was full of gaiety and life, a life well known to well-to-do families of the California countryside in the 'seventies and 'eighties.

In the late 'seventies, James Kelly bought the Lankershim Ranch and left Virginia City for good, not long after the great fire there and the death of his wife. There had been two James Kellys in the bonanza city: Whiskey Kelly and Soda Kelly. Soda was our man, proprietor of the Pioneer Soda Works. One must presume that, in keeping with his era, he had engaged also in the (sometimes) more lucrative enterprise, gambling in mining stocks, for he had piled up so substantial a fortune that he had retired from business and in Napa City henceforth was known as Bonanza Kelly. He had a numerous family, of daughters, chiefly.

All that I have been told about the Kelly family life and environment resembles my own childhood in the Piedmont of the 'eighties so closely that I might have lived in that old brick house myself. Like ours, it was a big household, with a dozen or a dozen and a half inmates according to the season: relative isolation in winter; in summer, incursions of visiting grandmothers or cousins or aunts. There was an abundance, indeed a superabundance, of "help"—one didn't call them servants unless one wanted to get their Irish up. For they were nearly all Irish, or if not Irish, they were Chinese. Many a time I have wondered where they all came from and where they all went to, the cartoon-type Irish of those days. There must have been a wholesale emigration from some poverty-stricken district in Ireland that flooded the labor markets in the little cities around San Francisco Bay. The men and women who cared for our cows and horses and chickens, raised our vegetables, churned our butter, cooked and laundered and nursemaided for us were all genial, gay, generous-minded folk, blue-eyed, with hair that was either very, very red or very, very black. (All except one: she was black-eyed and grim and warred with all the rest.) They served their time, sometimes brief, sometimes relatively long, as help to others, then, somehow, out of their pitiful wages they managed to save enough to start life for themselves on some little piece of ground. I have a strong suspicion that not infrequently the wicked paternalistic heads of families had their generous share in bringing about this release; but whether they did or not the ex-servitors nearly always remained the family's friends. Although we had worked them for scandalously long hours and for scandalously little pay, they named their children after us little devils who had teased wheelbarrow rides out of them and with surreptitious pebble-throwing had scared their placid cows into antimilking mood and sent hens squawking out of the henhouse before they laid their eggs. Californians hadn't heard, as yet, about the class war.

If one lived more than a mile or two out of town, a governess was more necessity than luxury. A few of the main roads had begun to be macadamized, but most of the lesser ones were still unpaved, dusty lanes in summer, quagmires in the rainy season. A public school might be from two to twenty miles away. How the children of men who farmed for a living ever got an education is hard to figure out. Many of them rode or walked eight or ten miles every day. One such child retained to the end of her life a hatred of California poppies—"and you'd hate them too," she grumbled, "if you'd had to walk three miles through the blinding glare of them five times a week and twice a day."

Sometimes one of the more public-spirited members of California's "snobocracy" would gather in the children of less opulent neighbors for schooling with his own brood. Such a semipublic, semiprivate school is said to have been held in Bonanza Kelly's granary for a while. Possibly these extra pupils were the children of men who tended his hayfields and milked his cows. He had no need to farm for a living. His ranch was made scrupulously productive, none the less, and was for the most part self-sustaining in the matter of food. Vegetables, fruit, berries, milk, butter, eggs; the chickens, turkeys, and ducks that became roasts and fricassees—all were grown on the place. Also the calves that were sent to the butcher now and again to be made into veal. One seldom found pigs on a pleasure ranch; they were held to be less genteel. Hams and sides of bacon, flour, sugar, and coffee were bought wholesale from Goldberg Bowen and Company and delivered at the ranch every three months, to the unrestrained joy of the children, bound in honor to pilfer a cake or two of chocolate from the delivery wagon under the blandly unobservant eyes of driver and help.

Certain times of the year had their ritualistic food responsibilities that all the children shared: the stoning of raisins for making mincemeat and plum puddings, the picking of currants for jelly and blackberries for jam—the sole reward for such labors the licking of jelly pots. Bread, biscuits, cakes, pies—all were homemade. Bread was baked several times a week and twenty loaves at a time. Fresh-baked bread and fresh-roasted coffee beans scented the big kitchen day after day. And one must not forget the sound of the ice-cream freezer grinding away—or being ground—outdoors under the linden tree, of a Sunday noon. And the early morning clash of iron stove lids in the big French range and the whirr of the coffee grinder that warned the drowsy child in the room above that breakfast, complete with fruit, oatmeal, bacon, eggs, and pancakes, was drawing near. The sounds and scents of the countryside remain the most poignant of memories: the lumbering wheels and screeching brakes on heavy wagons; the crowing of cocks and the loud cackling of hens; the smell of haycocks and barnyards, of flowering fruit trees and owl's clover; of tarweed and dusty roads and rain-soaked earth.

For months at a time, for the ranch family, society had to be as self-sustaining as the food. But with cherry season came a sure influx of visitors, invited or unexpected as might be. To Bonanza Kelly's they came from San Francisco to Vallejo by boat, thence along country roads, behind Kelly's fine span of horses if the visitor was in the first category, or drawn by some livery stable's nag if the notion to visit the ranch was all his own. In either case one's welcome was sure.

Although on some rainy afternoon in the next November, standing at a window and looking out on the wind-tossed cypress trees and the empty drive, daughter might mutter to daughter, "Wouldn't I like to see Johnny up in a cherry tree now!"

By that time the children were growing up, getting past the governess age. Finishing school, Mills Seminary most probably, loomed as the near destiny of daughter, prep school and college for son. This meant that, after Bonanza Kelly died—from after effects of a somewhat physical discussion with a hack driver, it is said—the ranch house was closed in wintertime. The permanent home became the summer home, used less and less as the years went by. For a generation now the house has been empty and silent the year round. A ghost of a house, its only epitaph is a sighing, "Nobody wants to live in it, but we can't bear to have it torn down."

13. NAPA SODA SPRINGS

When Gantt wrote to his friend Dr. Marsh that he felt "prematurely fashionable" in his patronage of the "Nappa" Valley hot springs, he was more of a prophet than he could have guessed. Barely thirty years later, three of the counties that had constituted General Vallejo's savage-infested northern frontier had become the fashionable vacation area for the families of San Francisco's wealthier pioneers. Hot springs and sulphur springs and iron springs and soda springs—all with health-giving attributes, it was held—were sprinkled over Sonoma and Lake and Napa counties as liberally as if ground out of a pepper pot. Skaggs Springs, Bartlett Springs, Adams, Seigler, Anderson, Mark West, the White Sulphur Springs, the Geysers, Calistoga—you "pays your money and you takes your choice."

Many of these resorts, however, were quite inaccessible. Bartlett's, for instance, or the Geysers entailed long, dusty, hot stage rides over steep and winding mountain roads that kept the lady passengers, duly swathed in veils and linen dusters, in paroxysms of terror. For a Lily Hitchcock such mad adventure might be all very well, but for San Francisco's upper crust, with its growing gentility, the Napa Valley was far more congenial.

The valley's accessibility offered another advantage, quite priceless in its way. Papa could deposit his family on a Saturday in a favorite resort—the family complete, with wife, children, governess, and nursemaid—and on Monday go back to town, to business as usual and a womanless state of being, most unusual, which probably seemed to him paradise itself. As it did to the Chinese cook, left in charge of the city house with only the boss's breakfast to cook and a lawn to water occasionally.

During the week, the older ladies at the springs could embroider and gossip to their heart's content, or hire carriages to drive them through the countryside, while the younger ones practiced their archery or played croquet to while away the hours until bachelors as well as patres familias were released again from business at the week's end. There would always remain a few beaux, however, who, while enjoying their own brief vacations, could greatly enhance the pleasure of the young ladies' more protracted sojourn. And protracted it was, indeed. None of this movement-mad business of flitting about from one resort to another, never spending two nights in the same bed. You chose your hotel and you "rusticated" there, sometimes for as long as two or three months. The cost was not prohibitive. Our chosen resort, one of the most elegant in the valley, advertised board and lodging at fifteen dollars a week.

The Napa Soda Springs did not come into prominence until the middle 'seventies, when Colonel J. P. Jackson was said to be planning "elegant and substantial" improvements. An earlier hotel, built in 1856, had burned down, and a long and bitter contest over property rights—"it is the greatest wonder that somebody was not killed," one chronicler states—kept it in the courts until the Land Commission could decide to whom it really did belong. Colonel Jackson then bought it. He was an Ohio man who had served in the Army of the Cumberland and under Grant. Later, he was in business in San Francisco, the owner of the *Daily Evening Post*, and was specially noted as an orator. Of one of his speeches it was said that it "will pass as a model of post-prandial felicity." And, the county historian further notes, "Ideality and causality are both leading qualities of his temperament."

Whether ideality or causality prompted Colonel Jackson's choice of an architect, his vast resort in the Napa Valley foothills became one of the wonders of the county, if not of the state. The Rotunda Hotel a pamphlet describes as "a magnificent structure . . . a circular building, towering up seventy-five feet into the air and surmounted by a huge glass cupola." Another writer directs one's attention particularly to the circular design, which caused the building to "comport with the natural surroundings. All of Nature's lines are curvilinear—and angles in the midst of Nature's work would be out of place."

As we read on, however, we grow a little confused. The writer all of a sudden is describing the stables, another—or is it the same?—"circular rotunda." Eighty stalls about its outer driveway, inside that again a bank for saddles which separates the driveway from the central carriage area. All the "painting and graining and all carpentry work . . . has been done with as much care . . . as though it were for a mansion for human beings of noble birth."

Yes, but where did the human guests sleep? We hear further of a skating rink, a basement wine cellar, and a clubhouse that was a "paragon of perfection," and of a special stable for guests who drove their own horses, and of the famous bottling works—a potpourri, indeed, of glass domes and horses and bottles, where the guest seems to have been singularly insignificant.

Turning again from the county history to a pamphlet frankly advertising the Napa Soda Springs, we find the Colonel's gift for language coming into its own. We learn specifically how to get to the Springs and what the cost will be, where and when we lunch and take the stagecoach, and then ". . . groves of oaks," we read, "gracefully festooned with immortal mistletoe, the tall and stately pine and the eucalyptus globulus . . . Lawns and flower-beds . . . with many shady nooks and cozy outlets . . . produce as lovely a spot as the tired business man with his family, or the invalid with his many ailments, could possibly find. The . . . Pagoda Spring . . . the Lemon Spring . . ." Among the attractions offered are lawn tennis and croquet, mountain drives and horseback rides, and as an ultimate boon, "Absence of all Noxious Vapors."

Nobody could ask for more, and nobody did. Everybody who was anybody sooner or later paid his visit to the Springs. We see them moving through the gardens in their best summer clothes—the ladies of course change their costumes three times a day. The guests unbend a little, perhaps, from the stiff requirements of the current etiquette. A young gentleman need not remind himself that "in bowing to a lady the hat is only lifted from the head, not held out at arm's length for a view of the interior," because in all probability he is carrying his hat under his arm, the better to duck under his fair companion's parasol for a glimpse of her modestly averted face. And in the complicated ritual of an introduction, perhaps some little margin of error may be permitted him. For in this hodgepodge resort society—unless he be Ned Greenway himself—how can he be expected instantly to "strike a balance of respect" between the relative positions of Mrs. X and Mrs. Z? What he had better remember, however, is that "in a ball-room, where the introduction is to dancing, not to friendship, you *never* shake hands, and as a general rule, an introduction is not followed by shaking hands, only by a bow . . . the more public the place of introduction, the less hand-shaking takes place."

The lady, too, is absolved from sundry rules, especially that puzzling one which says: "A lady never accompanies a gentleman to the door of the drawing-room . . . unless she has profound respect for him."

One wonders whether this rule was designed for the protection of the lady against a sudden onslaught in the hall, or to abet the growing feminine tendency to put man in his proper place. That objective was all very well in San Francisco, where men still outnumbered the women, but in a paradise virtually Adamless for the better part of the week, assuredly it was out of place.

Most of the old resort is gone now. Repeated fires have devastated it. Yet the ruins of a rotunda and of several other stone buildings still stand in grounds that retain some hint of their early magnificence. One building is intact—the Pagoda above the spring. Flanking it are Italian cypresses and imposing stone urns. In front of it stand a benign statue—perhaps the Goddess of Health—and a pair of stone dogs, mythology unknown. Shabby and unkempt though the Pagoda is, and though all the connotations of melancholy are present, somehow it suggests nothing but gaiety and youth. Along the paths that surround it children seem still to play their long-outmoded games: hoops and grace hoops and battledore and shuttlecock. Lovers take their prim and prissy ways along the lonelier paths that lead to the cozy nooks. And somewhere along the canyon road below the gardens, Papa is driving up from town—driving his own horses if his years and his fortunes permit, or, holding tight to his hat and aghast at the twelve-mile pace, riding behind a team urged to its speediest by the most ardent and eligible of his prospective sons-in-law.

14. WOODWARD'S GARDENS

◊ "What the Zoological Gardens are to London, the Jardin des Plantes to Paris, or the Central Park to New York, Woodward's Gardens are to San Francisco." So an advertisement in *The Wasp* of 1878 claims, not too extravagantly, for to a few old Californians, Woodward's Gardens were all that and indeed a great deal more. Although demolished half a century and more ago, they remain one's own little lost paradise, an unforgettable part of very early memories.

What does one remember? First of all, the rotary boat—sitting in it on a grownup's lap and by some mysterious agency being gently revolved around a little pond that had flowers floating on it. Later, one sat alone, in state, and watched the sails, and felt on one's face the wind that one now knew was what made the boat move. A band was playing in the high-arched stand near by. Flags and banners seem in recollection to have been streaming everywhere, though existing photographic evidence would limit them to the bear-borne flagstaffs outside the gate. But what does memory care about evidence? A child's cherished impressions of Woodward's need bear little relation to facts.

There *was* a pelican—"Alive, of course!" another child of that period maintains, though whether it was living or stuffed I myself cannot remember. It has blended with all other pelicans, or rather has become the apotheosis of all pelicans, as the goat cart has of goat carts. I think that the goat was white, but I know that to drive him was one of my unattained ambitions, for we left San Francisco before I grew up to him. The memory of him and of the riding camel instigated many a later experiment in the harnessing of patient dogs to gocarts and the saddling of calves. Not the people who swarmed the gardens, but the boat, the birds, stuffed or alive, and the animals—these are my Woodward's, even to the pink-eyed chocolate mouse on sale at the candy booth.

Of the man who created this child's paradise I have been able to learn very little. An item in San Francisco's *Alta California* of 1858 tells of a marvellous sweet potato on exhibition in the office of Robert B. Woodward's "What Cheer House" on Leidesdorff Street —a potato two and a half feet long weighing twelve and a half pounds. This early hint of a talent for showmanship is borne out by the form of Mr. Woodward's commercial advertisements. The good lodgings, advantageous prices, and free shower baths barely keep pace with the rarer attractions he offers: a library, a museum, and a reading room all free for his hotel's guests.

Already, it would seem, Mr. Woodward has the educational bee in his bonnet, though two years later the laying out of his garden has barely begun. By the end of the 'sixties he has visited the East and Europe and has started his collection of art treasures—which include Canova dancing girls, naturally. Not long afterward, his home on Mission Street, one unit of which is said to have been occupied by the Frémonts in early days, is thrown open to the public in a benefit for the Sanitary Commission. By 1873 an illustrated catalogue places the public in the gardens. Perhaps there, too, no less than in Warner's Menagerie, an Irishman stood amazed. "What can be plainer?" he mused. "First the monkey, then the rangey-tangey, then the nigger, and then the Irishman!"

Woodward's early proclaims itself far more than a mere amusement park. The catalogues give details of what the ambitious student may hope to gain from its exhibits: Marine Aquarium, Museum, Zoögraphicon—whatever that may be—Art Galleries, Conservatories, Menagerie, Seal and Fish Ponds, Amphitheatre, and Skating Rink. Nature, Art, and Science Illustrated. Admission 25 cents.

Moreover, its Amusement Department specializes in concerts, balls, festivals, national celebrations, balloon ascensions, tightrope walking and fireworks. Such wonderful fireworks! Roman candles, rockets, red fire, and "set pieces" such as Washington crossing the Delaware—that more often than not failed to set, but just sputtered and flared and died. The "spacious restaurant furnishes first-class meals at city prices"; the saloon offers "best qualities of wine, beer and cigars (no intoxicating liquors allowed to be served)."

The gardens by this time have been enlarged to include two whole city blocks. A tunnel under Fourteenth Street, connecting the two parts, is not the smallest factor in a child's entrancement. There is a picnic ground near the rotary boat. "The swings and gymnastic apparatus . . . goat-wagons (with a small extra charge), the camels for taking trips with loads of children, the circus trick-donkeys, the happy family cages, with frolicking monkeys, cats, dogs, pigs and raccoons . . ." The Mission Street horsecars will carry you to the gate, where, incidentally, lost children and lost articles are to be picked up.

Mrs. John Strentzel, in her diary of 1875, records going in October to the Gardens to see the Holy Ghost plant in full bloom. This orchid (*Peristeria elata*) resembles a white dove with extended wings. She notes other acquisitions: a new fernery, and "the stump that Captain Cook was killed under." A very eventful week, she further observes. The new Palace Hotel is giving its first banquet in honor of General Sheridan. One hopes that General Vallejo was an honored guest there, to tell his story of the coyotes that long years before sang their chorus on the spot where Adelina Patti was one day to find her bed and board.

Woodward's was not the only public garden in San Francisco, by any means. California has always had its outdoor amusements and resorts, from bearbaiting and bullfighting and strawberry-picnicking Spanish times down to the present. Furtive patrons swarmed the Willows (not far from Woodward's in the direction of Mission Dolores), rowdy crowds the Chutes or Shellmound Park (across the Bay); gay coaching parties drove to the races or to Del Monte—these and many another resort always were well attended. Yet among all those that existed before the earthquake and fire of 1906, the year when a new city was born, Woodward's was unique. It never was fashionable, and it never was tough. Grownups and children alike thronged it: Grandpa and Grandma on sunny benches in front of the bright flower beds; Papa with his beard and his truncated bowler hat; Mama in chignon, bustle, pelisse, and "short" skirt with dust ruffle that barely cleared the path; children white-stockinged, in little black buttoned boots, girls padded with layer after layer of petticoat, boys short-trousered, wearing ribbon-trimmed straw hats. There was a domestic quality about these holiday seekers, decent, decorous, almost strait-laced. Strange, but perhaps not wholly incredible, if this is as true a picture of the average San Franciscan as those so much oftener painted of Bonanza Palace and Barbary Coast.

Part Four

THE AGE OF MAGNIFICENCE

15. LINDEN TOWERS AND JAMES CLAIR FLOOD

The title Bonanza Kings, said to have been first bestowed upon those shrewd speculators, Messrs. Mackay, Fair, Flood, and O'Brien when the facts about their great strike in Virginia Consolidated at last leaked out, does not rank them quite as aptly now as it did seventy-five years ago. In the language of today, "bonanza" denotes something other than the dictionary definition, "a rich pocket of ore." It has also come to bear the connotation of sudden and unexpected luck. Our quartette's acquisition of a huge fortune most decidedly was not that.

For two years, while Fair and Mackay delved deep under Virginia City, Flood and O'Brien in San Francisco had been carrying on their planned share of the work. The secret of the great vein had been scrupulously kept. As modest proprietors of the Auction Lunch, engaged in cooking chowders and mixing drinks, they had made the most of their opportunity to listen to speculators' gossip and gather in, at their cheapest, as many "feet" of their fabulous mine as less well-informed gamblers could be prevailed upon to part with. The ultimate disclosure of this unsuspected wealth was sensational. San Francisco went even more mad than usual over bonanza silver. The name caught the popular fancy, so much so that the word bonanza has been kept alive, though its antithesis, *borrasca*, denoting a vein that has petered out, has been forgotten along with the names of those luckless gamblers who had sold their stock before the strike. The two words had still another definition in early days. A *bonanza* in sailor talk meant fair weather, and *borrasca*, a storm.

Fair and Mackay, Charles Shinn says, were expert silver miners; the Auction Lunch partners, speculators only, though as time went on, Flood developed outstanding financial talent. In New York, he had been a maker of carriages and wagons, an apprentice who had risen rapidly to be foreman of his shop. Wages for overtime in the frenzied business of building great wagons for overland travel supplied him with his own gold-seeker's stake. He sailed as a cabin passenger, by way of Panama, and arrived in California in 1849 with money in his pocket, a fact that he liked to dwell on in later life.

His early days in California followed much the usual pattern. He spent a relatively short time in mining, then returned to carriage building, a business that he understood. A year or two before the Nevada frenzy struck San Francisco, he and O'Brien opened their saloon and, at first in a small way, began to speculate in stock. By 1875 the four Irishmen had been crowned Bonanza Kings, had built their own Bank of Nevada, and had become an active threat to their competitor Ralston and his Bank of California.

After Flood's success in the stock market, he—or perhaps it was Mrs. Flood—was ready to turn attention to another current madness, the building of fantastic wooden palaces. His first mansion in San Francisco receives little comment, either for its architecture or for its site. "Every part of the city has a tinge of gentility," a social authority of the times states, though history now shows that South Park had already lost face somewhat and Nob Hill had not yet attained eminence. But the mark of a successful man now unquestionably is his country estate. Ralston's (later Sharon's) at Belmont, Milton Latham's at Palo Alto, D. O. Mills's at Millbrae, and not the least of these, James Flood's at Menlo Park.

Linden Towers was the formal name of the Flood mansion, though San Francisco's columnists preferred to call it Flood's Wedding Cake. It was situated, appropriately enough, on the Middlefield Road, for its master was a middling sort of man. Of middle height, "rather stout without being obese," and quiet of manner, Flood was liberal in his charities and liked that fact to be publicized. A man of few intimates, "little tolerant of placing his time at the disposal of people from whose society he could obtain no satisfactory quid pro quo." Quite an ordinary person, in fact; but not so his house.

The huge wooden structure must have covered some two acres of ground. Its architecture—"a modification of the Louis Quatorze," *Harper's Weekly* asserts—was indeed so far modified as to include almost every historical period except the Greek. Gothic, Renaissance, Romanesque, Lord-knows-what; round towers, square towers—every wing and wall flaunted a different style of decoration, fenestration, roof, balcony, and chimney top. Drawing rooms, ballrooms, music rooms—all were "furnished and decorated with as much taste as lavishness of outlay." Indeed, a study of the "chaste" appointments of Linden Towers would be "a liberal education in the minor arts subsidiary to architecture." Gracing the gardens was a sixty-foot fountain, and also an artificial lake stocked with game fishes. Twenty horses lived in luxury in a stable as well appointed as the house, and the polished floor of its carriage room alone was so large and so glassy that it might well have been used for a charity ball.

Among the many distinguished guests entertained at Linden Towers after its completion early in 1879, one at least must have come up to Flood's requirements in the matter of a *quid pro quo*—General Grant, who expressed boundless admiration for the vast palace. Gertrude Atherton's version of his visit there is piquant, though possibly not wholly authentic. The Flood installation at Menlo had been viewed with considerable displeasure by the Peninsula's Southern set. Whether calls should be made upon the family of a former saloonkeeper had become a very lively question. Grant's acceptance of an invitation to lunch at Linden Towers set the seal of approval on house and inmates alike.

Yet the occasion proved to the satisfaction of the the Peninsula that the Floods were outsiders, after all. It wasn't cricket, really, the trick that Mrs. Flood played on a neighbor. When she invited her lion to a quiet little lunch she chose the same day as the Senator's historic reception for him at Belmont. And the lion, stuffed and satiated with Linden Towers delicacies, as varied and recherché as the details of its architecture, proved more than a little lethargic in his roars that evening.

The Floods attended the reception, of course, and in regal panoply: Mrs. Flood in a black velvet court dress and Miss Jenny in white satin and a diamond tiara—a hint of the bridal in her splendor, as if taking cognizance of Ulysses Junior and sundry augurs of romance. Prematurely, however, as the story turned out—if there was a story. Jenny's alleged engagement to young Grant has survived only as rumor, one legend among many others about bonanza pageantry. That she was included a few days later in the party of debutantes that accompanied the Grants on their trip to Yosemite is confirmed by current newspaper accounts. Not so, the famous lunch. Of his meeting with the Floods, the only mention I found in the society columns is that Grant "attended a garden party at Linden Towers."

The apex of extravagance and senseless magnificence seems to have been reached in this visit of General Grant to San Francisco. Extravagance of course belonged to the period; it was not an attribute of San Francisco alone, though the mad speculation fever so long epidemic there may have been the initial stimulus. But San Franciscans, whether they loved the spectacle or whether they hated it, lapped up the accounts of frenzied magnificence with a gusto duly attested by the amount of space accorded by the weekly journals and daily newspapers. Although the *Wasp* sneers at our "snobocracy" and its imperial court with Mackay, Flood, and Stanford as its dukes, it nevertheless fills its columns with items about both Californian and European royalty. Lips are smacked over the report that Mrs. Mackay, never happy out of the shadow of the Arc de Triomphe, has spent more than $70,000 at the Paris Exposition. The Stanfords are soon to "startle the Gothamites by one of their princely receptions." And we are told, authoritatively, that James Flood's house is the most superb on our continent; indeed, "no royal or ducal house in Europe excels it."

A vague consciousness of objectives other than extravagant spending does disturb the general complacency now and again. San Francisco is beginning to cast a critical eye upon its past. "The moral taint which a few years since would have passed unobserved now acts as a bar to its innermost circle," the Social Manual of 1884 unctuously says. And again we find this neat summing up of San Francisco's progress in manners and mores: "The simple adventurer merged into the gambler, the gambler into the stock-sharp, the stock-sharp into the regular broker . . . until we reached the summit of wealthy leisure and unexceptional [sic] gentility."

The manual, however, is not infallible. With the history of the period open to the last page before us, we may be forgiven for suspecting that in the expression of its principal article of faith—"The reproach of the *nouveaux riches* is passing" from San Francisco—the manual, after all, was a bit premature.

16. ADOLPH SUTRO'S HOUSE

On an afternoon in the early 'eighties, Adolph Sutro and his daughter Emma, out driving together, turned the horses toward the cliffs above the ocean beach and came upon a white cottage set in a garden. "Never," said Sutro, "have I seen a view to equal this. If the house is for sale, I want it."

His knock at the door brought the owner of the cottage, who proved to be Samuel Tetlow, no less widely known in California than Adolph Sutro himself, though for far different reasons. Tetlow was the proprietor of the Bella Union, a saloon, gambling house, and theatre, long one of the most popular resorts in California. Never noted for its propriety, the Bella Union in the more decorous 'seventies had lost caste. Attendance there had sharply declined, and Tetlow's financial position induced him to accept Sutro's offer. "Within a few hours," a family record reads, "Sutro had possession of the property."

That surrender of Tetlow's might be regarded as

some endorsement of the *Social Manual*'s contentions about San Francisco's growing gentility. The hell-roaring city really was on the downgrade; and on the slide with it, though this was as yet barely apparent, was the era of gimcrack palaces and wild speculation. Men and women alike were beginning to think more earnestly in terms of civic responsibility. Society women, by means of bazaars and fetes and charity balls were making awareness of poverty and of the ills of destitute children quite fashionable. The Sanitary Commission had society's backing, as had the idea of a social settlement. In short, wealth was beginning to rub eyes awake to the first faint dawn of what we like to call a social consciousness.

Of all San Francisco's bonanza millionaires, Adolph Sutro best represented the new trend. His long battle against Ralston had developed into a fight for human rights and decencies as against corporate greed. In his vast project of tunneling under Mount Davidson, Sutro took the novel stand that the miners' safety might be just as important as the stockholders' pocketbooks. Ralston also, it is true, had had his dreams of progress and betterment. His aim was a greater San Francisco—and with it, perhaps, a greater Ralston. He had worked ceaselessly to found industries, had organized a bank, and had endorsed a great railway system. He could be kind and generous. Out of his own pocket he endowed the widow of a ruined friend who had committed suicide; but he never allowed kindliness to interfere with his personal success.

Sutro was a man of quite different caliber. In the seventeen years that he spent in battering down opposition to his famous tunnel and carrying the work to a successful conclusion against incredible odds—unpredictable odds such as the Franco-Prussian War, which put an end to any financial help from Europe's banks, or the impeachment of Andrew Johnson, which blocked Congressional action—it was not only for the success of a business enterprise that he fought. His finished tunnel would mean immense improvement in the working conditions of thousands of miners who had long suffered from choking heat in the miles upon miles of Comstock shafts and had been exposed to constant danger from flood and fire.

Sutro's beginnings had been less humble than those of many Californians. His had been a well-to-do manufacturing family in Aix-la-Chapelle. From childhood he had known cultured people and attractive surroundings. But at sixteen he had had to leave school to become superintendent of his father's factory; and two years later, revolution ended prosperity and sent the family to America.

The young Adolph arrived in San Francisco in 1851. Five years afterward, when he married, he was still a cigar dealer and still in modest circumstances. In a few years more, however, his great dream began to assume shape, and he himself emerged into public notice—a controversial figure, alternately applauded and derided; favored by the Ralston powers, savagely opposed by them; at one time virtually outlawed by the financiers, at another granted millions in loans by great European banks. At last, in 1875, his tunnel penetrated to the Savage mine, and the threat of underground floods was ended on the Comstock.

To most self-taught men a mastery of mining engineering would seem achievement enough for a lifetime. Sutro did not rest content with that. After selling out his interest in the tunnel, he retired to San Francisco and invested in land—acres and acres of bald dunes between the Western Addition and the ocean. He planted Sutro Forest and built Sutro Baths. To the University of California he gave land for its Affiliated Colleges. He founded a great library. And against the opposition of all the newspapers, distrustful of his sympathy with the cause of labor and his tolerance of the hated and feared Dennis Kearney, he was elected mayor of San Francisco.

Of all these projects, however, his house and garden above the ocean soon became dearest to him. Twenty acres of land went with the Tetlow cottage. Into the development of his gardens Sutro put all of the push and drive and enthusiasm that had carried him to his Comstock victory. Trees, shrubbery, lawns, great stone terraces graced the cliffs and dunes. Compared with the palaces of other bonanza or railroad kings the house and its furnishings remained fairly simple; but the inevitable florescence of the period found expression in the statues that thronged the gardens. From the Venus de Milo and the Laocoön to the latest fashion in Canova dancing girls, replicas in stone, shipped from Italy in ballast, stood on pedestals in glades, lined avenues, rimmed terraces, even clung precariously to crevices in the cliffs. And the astonishing result was a garden of surpassing charm. Even when the ocean fog shrouded the great cypress avenue beyond the lion-guarded gates—perhaps then most of all—one wandered about entranced. The past was romantically summed up in that extravagant garden, so true was it to its period. San Francisco suffered an irreparable loss when its authorities wrecked the historic house, which had been willed to the city by the Sutro family, and allowed the gardens to run to waste. Even though a conscientious Art Commission may have worried about exposing public taste to a now-derided period of art, it might have paused to wonder what the public of seventy-five years hence is going to think of current art collections—paused, and perhaps stayed its hand.

From earliest days in Virginia City, Sutro had been a famous host. No housekeeping difficulties—and they abounded—could long stand in the way of maintaining the prestige of the Sutro hospitality or of the Sutro table. Since there were no markets near, he devised a market cart fitted with champagne baskets well lined with oilcloth to exclude the dust of the long drive to downtown San Francisco. His was the only residence for miles around, only a few scattered houses having been built as yet west of Presidio Avenue. The roads were heavy with sand, and unlighted. To illuminate Sutro's house, candles and kerosene lamps, long outmoded, had to suffice. But the fame of his breakfasts did not diminish, or the variety or distinction of his guests. "On one day he would entertain the astronomers from the Lick Observatory. On another he would open the heights to kindergarten children shepherded by Kate Douglas Wiggin . . . Dennis Kearney, the incendiary socialist and sand-lot orator . . . would be another guest, followed by

Andrew Carnegie . . . to discuss library problems." Or it might be Oscar Wilde, lecturing and being lionized in San Francisco, or Joaquin Miller, or William Jennings Bryan.

Yet with all this, his secretary further noted, "his daily life was ordered with the utmost simplicity." It was still a busy life, for Sutro held a firm rein on all his projects, and his agents looked to him for instructions in all the daily routine. Yet unlike many of the men who had fought and envied him, he knew how to enjoy leisure, how to make time for his beloved books, for long drives about his estate and slow strolls through his gardens. One of the outstanding Americans of his day, he remained at heart the cultivated European. Retirement to him meant not boredom and banishment from all that had made life interesting, but a rich and rewarding period toward which all his years of work had consciously been bent.

17. TWO QUEENS AND THEIR CASTLES

Kings loom rather large in California history. Railroad kings and bonanza kings and cattle kings all have played their part in shaping the state's destiny. Of their wives, however, comparatively little has been recorded, and of that a large part is society gossip in the weeklies and the daily newspapers of their times. Perhaps there was little to tell about most of them, apart from their regal magnificence. A great deal of the comment centers in their silks and velvets, their diamonds and rubies, their houses and opera boxes, and the menus offered at their receptions and dinners and kettledrums.

The menus, certainly, if not always the ladies, were worthy of going down in history. Even a Rockefeller today might shrink from the cost of one wedding breakfast. That light repast included oysters, consommé, chicken and shrimp mayonnaise, varied cold meats and poultry, fancy sandwiches, sweetbread patties, filet with fresh mushrooms and green peas, fricassee of chicken, Charlotte Russe, ice cream, fancy cakes, wedding cake, bridecake, fruits, candies, bonbons, mottoes. And the beverages were claret, claret punch, iced lemonade, coffee, and champagne. The menu cards were of white plush fringed with silk and had a silver wedding bell on the front cover. The bride, overlooked until the last paragraph, wore white satin, duchesse lace, and diamonds. And the guests—this of course was before Ned Greenway got around to cataloguing the city's best—the guests were listed by the hundreds. Indeed, thousands could be mustered on occasion. Senator Sharon is said to have invited two thousand eminent citizens to Belmont to honor General Grant.

A place in San Francisco society at that time was not very difficult to attain—if one had the money. Ward McAllister had not yet been consecrated as an authority, and how much a San Franciscan could spend in entertainment was much more important than how he spent it. Nobody had ever told a bonanza king that it is in "excessive bad taste . . . to in any way refer to the cost of these dinners, balls, etc. Every one in society knows how to estimate such things." So he told the newspapers, copiously, how much everything cost, particularly his house. A bonanza king's crudities could be forgiven—in San Francisco. In New York, McAllister notes, "The launching of a beautiful girl into society is one thing: it is another to place her family on a good, sound social footing. You can launch them into the social sea, but can they float?" San Franciscans could. With them, self-esteem was a life raft that bore them triumphantly to any port.

The origins of our two queens, Jane Lathrop Stanford and Mary Sherwood Hopkins, had been equally unremarkable. Both began married life in Sacramento in a very small way, doing their own cooking and housework. In the quest for fortunes their husbands had both chosen business rather than mining. Mark Hopkins had been a grocer's clerk in an eastern village and may also have made some study of law. Leland Stanford, a farmer's son, had studied and practiced law in Wisconsin. The business of providing food for the miners, however, attracted the future partners. As early as 1849, Hopkins drove his own ox team from Sacramento to Placerville with groceries to open a store. He was worth only a modest $9,700 a decade later, Bancroft claims, when he joined with Theodore Judah and his associates, the Big Four, to organize the transcontinental railroad. Stanford, in partnership with his elder brother Josiah, had amassed many times that sum, though Huntington had even less. "Their audacity," says Bancroft, "appears an act of madness or of inspiration."

The Stanfords had early moved into prominence. In 1850, Leland and his partner, Nicholas Smith, had taken turns as night watchman, sleeping, covered with buffalo robes, on the counter of their store, one arm dangling down so that, if the floodwaters reached the sleeper's fingertips, he would wake up and save the stock. Ten years later, with a sound fortune to buttress him, Stanford took time off from business to enter politics and was elected governor. Floods still pursued him. The levees overflowed. To get to the Capitol at 7th and I streets on the day of his inauguration he had to row there in a boat. That evening the Governor and his wife were serenaded. The boatloads of caroling citizens made them think of Venice, they said. Perhaps in that gratifying moment Leland was remembering his first store and the plop of the priceless sugar bags as the sugar in the bottom ones melted and the top ones fell into the flood.

Leland and Jane had long since left their frugal cottage on Second Street and had bought the far more pretentious house on Eighth and N. The walls and ceilings of its elegant parlors were adorned with as many different kinds of plaster of Paris sculpture as the most prolific decorator could slap on. At a ball honoring Governor Booth, given there in the spring of 1872, "6,000 square feet of space" was "covered with the tireless dancers." So, at least, the San Francisco *Chronicle* boasts, as proudly as if of its own; for the Stanfords were about to leave Sacramento's lesser grandeur and pass on to the more monumental splendor in San Francisco.

Mary Hopkins, in the meantime, had not been doing so well. Her Mark had likewise prospered, and at the completion of the railroad he too was a very rich man. He had, however, none of Leland's flair for magnificence. He was older, for one thing, constitutionally frugal and abstemious, shunning distinction as much as Stanford courted it. "A most competent and correct business man," his obituary in the *Alta California* frostily reads. "He was a hard worker, and it might almost be said that he had no enjoyment save in his work. He was quiet, unpretending, affable . . ." His death in Yuma in March, 1878, hardly raises a ripple of interest in the newspapers. This seems particularly strange, since his great chateau on Nob Hill was at that time racing to a finish alongside Leland Stanford's more restrained but no less magnificent mansion. The exterior, at least, of Leland's redwood castle bore no foreign taint: it was pure bonanza San Francisco.

The chateau, of course, was Mary's doing, not Mark's. He had never dreamed what would be let loose in that quiet little spouse of his once he had given in to her notion that his fortune, no less than Leland's, was worthy of, indeed exacted, a fine new house. He may not have known very much about her at all, in fact. Theirs reads like a rather tepid romance. They were first cousins, and Mary, even in the early days of her marriage, was restless, making long visits to her girlhood home in New England. They had no children. Timothy Hopkins was an adopted son, more cherished by Mark than by Mary it would seem in the light of her eventual disinheritance of him. An intensive reading of novels of the Ouida type was her one concession to romance—at least until she met Edward Searles—and the novels seemingly were the inspiration of her vast pinnacled and towered and fantastically decorated house.

Perhaps it was just as well for Mark that he never had to live in that house. Few people ever did, for long. It was a gesture rather than a residence, designed chiefly, one may surmise, to put Jane Stanford in her place. In wooden towers and Gothic sculpture (machine-sawed out of wood), as well as in the great stone bastions that buttressed its lawns, it far surpassed its neighbor. Grandiose occasions are reported —a fancy-dress cotillion in which Miss Flood looked the Spanish gypsy to perfection; a ball honoring Mary's niece, Clara Crittenden; Clara's marriage to Timothy Hopkins; a crowning evening when the mansion "donned its festive garb of exotics and an atmosphere of illumination and music pervaded the apartments so rich in upholstery and works of art." After a few years of this, however, the widow tired of San Francisco, married a new husband, and departed for Massachusetts and the building of still another great chateau.

Next door to the Hopkins house in San Francisco, the preposterous Stanford mansion with its forty rooms, no two of them alike in color, furnishing, or mode, fared a little better, but not very much so. The young Leland, for whose future social splendor the house had chiefly been planned, enjoyed only one great party there with friends of his own age. After the boy's death his father lost interest in the house and spent more and more time at his place down the Peninsula. The Nob Hill palace had its dinners and receptions nonetheless. The wonderful "orchestrion" rendered its operatic music, and the artificial birds on the tree in the central hall came to life at the push of a button and duly teetered and twittered and sang. Included in the decorations of the Pompeian Room, where Jane stood to receive guests, was a slab of onyx that once had adorned a defective pillar in St. Peter's in Rome. And the dinners! At one given for Miss

Crocker and Charles Alexander the central decoration of the dining table was a large silver epergne "adorned with Baltimore Belle and La France roses caught up by festoons of lavender and pink pearl-edged baby ribbon." Smaller epergnes held wistaria, banksia roses, and wild grasses—trembling, one suspects, at finding themselves in such elegant and cultivated company. For, beside the plates and the little bouquets of Maréchal Niel roses and Quaker lilies—tied with ribbons—and the bonbons—in ribbons—were placed hand-painted menu cards inscribed with appropriate quotations from Shakespeare.

Did Mary Hopkins, now Mary Searles, read about all this splendor in her own splendid New England retreat? Read it and envy Jane her eminence? At least she was spared the ordeal of watching Jane's triumphant career as widow, for Mary died in the summer of 1891, before Mark's colleague Leland did. She had permanently closed the Nob Hill chateau some months before and had gone back East to the unimposing husband, twenty-five years her junior, whose sole claims to attention seem to have been his marriage to "the richest woman in the world" and a passion that he, like Sir George Sitwell, indulged in to excess—the rearrangement of the household furniture. Perhaps in the last week of Mary's life, as she drove impassively along the New England roads, "a sad face behind the curtains of her carriage," she was thinking of early friendships and later rivalries—thinking of Mrs. Mackay, who had just entertained a Royal Princess and a Royal Duke in London, and had engaged Emma Eames to sing for them. Why,

Mary may have wondered, did the Mackay woman and the Stanford woman get so much notice in the newspapers, while she, with her wealth and her castles and her young husband hardly ever appeared in them at all?

One last bid for notoriety remained—a funeral. If Mary could not hope to rival the pageantry of Jane's son's funeral train in its regal progress across the continent, still there was a fifteen-thousand-dollar granite vault and a blue-satin-covered coffin to be talked about. There were guards dressed like monks, to keep a curious public from invading the grounds—only the public did not come. A few more newspaper paragraphs, about Mary's will chiefly, and the bitter injustice of it, and the universal hope that Timothy Hopkins would contest it—and Mary is forgotten.

Perhaps it would have been some gratification to her could she have known that neighbor Jane, as widow, was to have her share of adverse criticism. Jane never lacked publicity. Her firm hand on the young and struggling Stanford University, if nothing else, would have kept her in the public eye. But as time went on, there were whispered comments on her increasing eccentricity. Spiritualism, it was said, was becoming an obsession. Outwardly all her energies were bent on carrying out to the last detail the least of her husband's wishes. It was Victoria and Albert all over again. Secretly, however, she was finding increasing satisfaction in setting her own judgment against his. A grotesque little event illustrates this. Leland, to honor some cherished guest, used to plant a tree in his Palo Alto garden and would duly label it with the guest's name. Jane took a dislike to one man so commemorated, and after Leland's death removed the label from the tree. A gardener replaced it. That night Jane commanded her secretary's services in the garden, and together they hacked down the tree—a sapling still, one hopes—and dragged it out of sight.

Belief in her own power, her command over people's destinies, and in Heaven's approval of that power became another obsession. When displeased with any person or any course of events she would stop short in her tracks, her secretary says, and aloud, in peremptory manner, ask God what he thought or meant to do about it. She did not live to see the end of her era. She was spared knowledge of the holocaust which wiped out that symbol of her times, the group of bonanza palaces on Nob Hill. Yet it is not hard to imagine a proud, grim little ghost hovering near the palaces on that night in 1906, watching the flames lick toward them, seeing them vanish forever behind the smoke. A ghost not cowed, not impotent, scarcely even grieved. Merely annoyed. "Really, God!" she says in sharp reproof. "*Really!* Is this—necessary?"

SOURCES

CHAPTER 1: Fort Ross, a Count, and a Princess

The quotations in this chapter are from Eugène Duflot de Mofras (Marguerite Eyer Wilbur, tr.), *Duflot de Mofras' Travels on the Pacific Coast* (2 vols.; Santa Ana, Calif., The Fine Arts Press, 1937), II, 7, 10, 168; Hubert Howe Bancroft, *History of California* (7 vols.; San Francisco, 1884–1890), IV, 249 n.; Nellie Van de Grift Sanchez, *Spanish Arcadia* (San Francisco, Powell Publishing Company, 1929), pp. 124–125 (quotations used by permission of Louis Sánchez, owner of the author's rights); Gertrude Atherton, "The Romance of Fort Ross," *Californian Illustrated Magazine*, V (1893), 57–62, pp. 62, 61.

In addition to the works listed above, the following were used as sources: Auguste Bernard du Hautcilly, *Voyage autour du monde, principalement à la Californie* (2 vols.; Paris, 1834–1835); idem (Charles Franklin Carter, tr.), "Duhaut-Cilly's Account of California in the Years 1827–28," *California Historical Society Quarterly*, VIII (1929) 130–166, 214–250, 306–366; William Heath Davis, *Seventy-five Years in California* (San Francisco, John Howell, 1929); Eugène Duflot de Mofras, *Exploration du territoire de l'Orégon, des Californies et de la Mer Vermeille* (Paris, 1844); E. O. Essig, "The Russian Settlement at Ross," *California Historical Society Quarterly*, XII (1933), 191–209; *History of Marin*

OLD CALIFORNIA HOUSES

County, California (San Francisco, Alley, Bowen & Co., 1880); George D. Lyman, *John Marsh, Pioneer* (New York, Charles Scribner's Sons, 1931); Myrtle McKittrick, V*allejo, Son of California* (Portland, Ore., Binfords & Mort, 1944); Honoria Tuomey, *History of Sonoma County, California* (2 vols.; San Francisco, The S. J. Clarke Publishing Company, 1926).

CHAPTER 2: The Petaluma Adobe and General Vallejo

The quotations are from Rufus Kay Wyllys, "French Imperialists in California," *California Historical Society Quarterly*, VIII (1929), 116–129, p. 121 (quotations from this publication used by permission of the publisher: California Historical Society); Nellie Van de Grift Sanchez, *Spanish Arcadia*, pp. 279–282; Platón Vallejo, quoted in James H. Wilkins, "Memoirs of the Vallejos," San Francisco *Bulletin*, Jan. 28, 1914; Guadalupe Vallejo, "Ranch and Mission Days in Alta California," *Century Magazine*, XLI (Dec., 1890), 183–192, p. 185; H. H. Bancroft, *History of California*, III, 19 n.; Myrtle McKittrick, V*allejo, Son of California* (Portland, Ore., 1944), p. 348 (quotations used by permission of the publisher: Binfords & Mort).

Additional sources: H. H. Bancroft, *California Pastoral* (San Francisco, 1888); Jacob N. Bowman, "Adobes of the San Francisco Bay Area" (MS, Bancroft Library); Alice Mae Cleaveland, "The North Bay Shore During the Spanish and Mexican Regimes" (M.A. thesis, University of California, 1932, MS, Bancroft Library); W. H. Davis, *Seventy-five Years in California*; Myrtle Garrison, *Romance & History of the California Ranchos* (San Francisco, Harr Wagner Publishing Company, 1935); Celeste G. Murphy, *The People of the Pueblo* (Sonoma, W. L. and C. G. Murphy, 1935); Charles Howard Shinn, "Pioneer Spanish Families in California," *Century Magazine*, XLI (Jan., 1891), 377–389; Bayard Taylor, *Eldorado; or, Adventures in the Path of Empire* (2 vols.; New York, 1850); George Tays, "Mariano Guadalupe Vallejo and Sonoma," *California Historical Society Quarterly*, XVI (1937), 99–121, 216–254, 348–372, XVII (1938), 50–73, 141–167, 219–242.

PORTRAITS AND STORIES

CHAPTER 3: Victor Castro's Adobe

The quotations are from J. N. Bowman, "Adobes of the San Francisco Bay Area"; *Contra Costa Gazette*, July 7, 1860; Auguste Bernard du Hautcilly (Carter, tr.), "Duhaut-Cilly's Account of California in the Years 1827–28," *California Historical Society Quarterly*, VIII, 243; H. H. Bancroft, *History of California*, II, 755; San Francisco *Californian*, Dec. 29, 1847; *History of Contra Costa Co., California* (San Francisco, W. A. Slocum & Co., 1882), p. 114.

Additional sources: H. H. Bancroft, *California Pastoral*; idem, *History of California*, III, 583-584; Herbert Eugene Bolton, *Fray Juan Crespi* (Berkeley, University of California Press, 1927); Alice Mae Cleaveland, "The North Bay Shore During the Spanish and Mexican Regimes"; W. H. Davis, *Seventy-five Years in California*; Myrtle Garrison, *Romance & History of the California Ranchos*; F. J. Hulaniski, *History of Contra Costa County* (Berkeley, 1917); Mae Fisher Purcell, *History of Contra Costa County* (Berkeley, The Gillick Press, 1940); John Francis Sheehan, "The Story of the San Pablo Rancho," *Overland Monthly*, XXIV (Nov., 1894), 517–523; William A. Streeter, "Recollections of Historical Events in California," *California Historical Society Quarterly*, XVIII (1939), 64–71, 157–179, 254–278; George Tays, "Mariano Guadalupe Vallejo and Sonoma," *California Historical Society Quarterly*, Vols. XVI and XVII.

CHAPTER 4: A Martínez Adobe

The quotations are from "The Martínez Family," Bancroft Scraps (MS, Bancroft Library); José Arnaz, "Recuerdos" (MS, Bancroft Library, 1878), p. 44; Auguste Bernard du Hautcilly, *Voyage autour du monde*, I, 310–312; idem (Carter, tr.), "Duhaut-Cilly's Account of California in the Years 1827–28," *California Historical Society Quarterly*, VIII, 140, 141; J. N. Bowman, "Adobes of the San Francisco Bay Area"; Carmel Grace Martínez, "Don Ignacio Martínez," *Pony Express Courier*, X (Sept., 1943), 3; W. H. Davis, *Seventy-five Years in California* (San Francisco, 1929), pp. 70, 180 (quotations used by permission of the publisher: John Howell); H. H. Bancroft, *History of California*, II, 692; Brigida Briones, in *Century Magazine*, XLI (Jan., 1891), 470; *Contra Costa Gazette*, June 23, 1860; Guadalupe Vallejo, "Ranch and Mission Days in Alta California," *Century Magazine*, XLI (Dec., 1890), 183–192, p. 191.

Additional sources: H. H. Bancroft, *California Pastoral*; Eugène Duflot de Mofras, *Exploration du territoire de l'Orégon, des Californies et de la Mer Vermeille*; Zoeth S. Eldredge, *The Beginnings of San Francisco* (2 vols.; San Francisco, 1912); Myrtle Garrison, *Romance & History of the California Ranchos*; Deed: Abelino and Encarnación Altamirano to John Strentzel, 1850, in Contra Costa County Courthouse; conversations with George Griffin, Frank Swett, and Carmel Martínez (great-great-granddaughter of Ignacio Martínez).

CHAPTER 5: Rancho Monte del Diablo

The quotations are from the *Contra Costa Gazette*, May 12, 26, 1860; H. H. Bancroft, "Personal Observations of a Tour of the Missions in California" (MS, Bancroft Library, 1874), pp. 122, 126–130.

Additional sources: H. H. Bancroft, *California Pastoral*, p. 420; *idem*, *History of California*, III, 27; VI, 663; Annie Loucks, "Early History of Pacheco, Contra Costa County, California" (mimeographed, Pacheco, 1939); *San Francisco Call*, Aug. 15, 1876; newspapers, clippings, etc., in the possession of Mrs. F. C. Galindo; oral accounts from Mr. William E. Colby, Mrs. F. C. Galindo, and Mr. George Griffin.

CHAPTER 6: The Stone House and John Marsh

The quotations are from the *San Francisco Bulletin*, July 19, Sept. 26, 1856; H. H. Bancroft, *History of California*, VI, 10–11; Emily June Ulsh, "Doctor John Marsh, California Pioneer, 1836–1856" (M.A. thesis, University of California, 1924), pp. 99, 188–189; William H. Brewer (Francis P. Farquhar, ed.) *Up and Down California in 1860–1864* (New Haven, Yale University Press, 1931), p. 272.

PORTRAITS AND STORIES

Additional sources: H. H. Bancroft, *History of California*; J. N. Bowman, "Adobes of the San Francisco Bay Area"; G. D. Lyman, *John Marsh, Pioneer*.

CHAPTER 7: John Strentzel and John Muir

The quotations are from conversations with John Muir (1914) and Frank Swett.
Additional sources: William F. Badè, *The Life and Letters of John Muir* (2 vols.; Boston and New York, Houghton Mifflin Company, 1924), pp. 122, 117; H. H. Bancroft, *Chronicles of the Builders of the Commonwealth* (7 vols.; 1891–1892); *History of Contra Costa County* (San Francisco, W. A. Slocum & Co., 1882); Linnie Marsh Wolfe, *Son of the Wilderness: The Life of John Muir* (New York, A. A. Knopf, 1945); *Contra Costa Gazette*, 1860–1865, *passim*.

CHAPTER 8: John Bidwell's House

The quotations are from a letter written by Dr. Harrington B. Graham to the author, May 15, 1950; H. H. Bancroft, *History of California*, IV, 269.
Additional sources: John Bidwell, *Echoes of the Past* (Chicago, R. R. Donnelly Sons Co., 1928); Cora Edith Cody, "John Bidwell; His Early Career in California" (M.A. thesis, University of California, 1927); Julian Dana, *Sutter of California* (New York, Press of the Pioneers, 1934); Rockwell D. Hunt, *John Bidwell, Prince of California Pioneers* (Caldwell, Idaho, The Caxton Printers, 1942).

CHAPTER 9: A Graveyard and a School

The quotations are from A. A. Sargent, "Sketch of Nevada County," in Brown and Dallison, *Nevada and Grass Valley and Rough and Ready Directory* (San Francisco, 1857); Bayard Taylor, *Eldorado, or, Adventures in the Path of Empire*, I, 223; San Francisco *Californian*, Oct. 27, 1847 (extract from the New York *Tribune*, Apr. 30); Daniel Lévy, *Les Français*

OLD CALIFORNIA HOUSES

en Californie (San Francisco, 1884), pp. 32–33; C. H. Shinn, *Mining Camps: A Study in Frontier Government* (New York, 1885), pp. 134–135; Edna Bryan Buckbee, *The Saga of Old Tuolumne* (New York, 1935), p. 100 (quotation used by permission of the publisher: Press of the Pioneers); Frank Marryat, *Mountains and Molehills; or, Recollections of a Burnt Journal* (New York, 1855), p. 229; San Francisco *Alta California*, July 20, 1853.

Additional sources: H. H. Bancroft, *Popular Tribunals* (2 vols.; San Francisco, 1887); Julian Dana, *Lost Springtime: The Chronicle of a Journey, Far Away and Long Ago* (New York, The Macmillan Company, 1938); *A Memorial and Biographical History of the Counties of Merced, Stanislaus, Calaveras, Tuolumne and Mariposa, California* (Chicago, The Lewis Publishing Co., 1892); Hero Eugene Rensch, "History of California Mining Districts: Columbia, a Gold Camp of Old Tuolumne" (mimeographed, Berkeley, 1936), pp. 32–33; Josiah Royce, *California, from the Conquest in 1846 to the Second Vigilance Committee* (Boston and New York, 1886); Sarah Royce, *A Frontier Lady: Recollections of the Gold Rush and Early California* (New Haven, Yale University Press, 1932); Columbia *Times*, Jan. 12, 1860; San Francisco *Alta California*, July 20, 1853; San Francisco *Californian*, July 31, 1847; *Grizzly Bear Magazine*, Vol. III. No. 6 (Oct., 1908), p. 7, quoted from an unnamed source of fifty years earlier.

CHAPTER 10: Chez Pellaton

The quotations are from H. H. Bancroft, *Popular Tribunals*, I, 467; Daniel Lévy, *Les Français en Californie*, pp. 67, 71–72, 93–95 (translations by M.R.P.).

Additional sources: Hero Eugene Rensch, "History of California Mining Districts: Columbia"; Louis J. Stellman, *Mother Lode: The Story of California's Gold Rush* (San Francisco, Harr Wagner Publishing Company, 1934); Edward Vischer, "A Trip to the Mining Regions in the Spring of 1859," *California Historical Society Quarterly*, XI (1932), 224–226, 321–328; Henry L. Walsh, *Hallowed Were the Gold Dust Trails: The Story of the Pioneer Priests of Northern*

PORTRAITS AND STORIES

California (Santa Clara, Calif., University of Santa Clara Press, 1947); Otheto Weston, *Mother Lode Album* (Stanford, Calif., Stanford University Press, 1948); Richard Coke Wood, *Tales of Old Calaveras* (Angel's, Calif., Calaveras Californian, 1949).

CHAPTER 11: A Parish Church

The quotations are from *History of Nevada County, California* (Oakland, Thompson & West, 1880), p. 87; Charles E. De Long (Carl I. Wheat, ed.), "California's Bantam Cock," *California Historical Society Quarterly*, VIII (1939), 203; *Hesperian*, May 1, July 15, 1858.
Additional sources: *The Catholic Encyclopedia* (New York, Robert Appleton Co., 1907); Robert Nile, "Early-Day Mountain Freighting," *Journal of the Nevada County Historical Society*, October, 1950; H. L. Walsh, *Hallowed Were the Gold Dust Trails*; Nevada *Weekly Gazette*, 1867; North San Juan *Times*, July 3, 1875.

CHAPTER 12: Bonanza Kelly's Ranch House

The quotation is from a conversation with Mrs. Edna F. Spencer.
Additional sources: Virginia City *Enterprise*, 1872 (various issues); conversations with Mrs. William F. Kelly and Mr. Henley Davis; personal recollections.

CHAPTER 13: Napa Soda Springs

The quotations are from Emily June Ulsh, "Doctor John Marsh, California Pioneer, 1836–1856," p. 188; *Napa Soda Springs: The Famous Mountain Resort . . . Jackson & Wooster, Proprietors* (San Francisco, 1890?), pp. 7, 3–5; *History of Napa and Lake Counties, California* (San Francisco, Slocum, Bowen & Co., 1881), pp. 294–297, 493–494; *A Social Manual for San Francisco and Oakland* (San Francisco, 1884), pp. 226–230.

OLD CALIFORNIA HOUSES

CHAPTER 14: Woodward's Gardens

The quotations are from an advertisement of Woodward's Gardens, in the *Wasp*, Apr. 20, 1878, *et seq.*; San Francisco *News Letter*, Oct. 18, 1873; *Illustrated Guide and Catalogue of Woodward's Gardens* (San Francisco, 1879), pp. 1-2; diary of Mrs. John Strentzel, Oct., 1875, in the possession of Mrs. Jean de Lipka, granddaughter of John Muir.

Additional sources: *Illustrated Guide and Catalogue of Woodward's Gardens* (San Francisco, 1873); San Francisco *Alta California*, Oct. 22, 1858.

CHAPTER 15: Linden Towers and James Clair Flood

The quotations are from *The Elite Directory for San Francisco and Oakland* (San Francisco, 1879), p. 20; *A Social Manual for San Francisco and Oakland* (1884), p. 22; *Memorial of James C. Flood* (San Francisco, Society of California Pioneers, 1889), p. 12; *Harper's Weekly*, Mar. 22, 1879; San Francisco *Argonaut*, Jan. 6, 1883.

Additional sources: Gertrude Atherton, *My San Francisco; a Wayward Biography* (New York, The Bobbs-Merrill Company, 1946); H. H. Bancroft, *History of Nevada, Colorado, and Wyoming* (San Francisco, 1890); Oscar Lewis, *Silver Kings: The Lives and Times of Mackay, Fair, Flood, and O'Brien* (New York, A. A. Knopf, 1947); G. D. Lyman, *Ralston's Ring; Californians Plunder the Comstock Lode* (New York, Charles Scribner's Sons, 1937); C. H. Shinn, *The Story of the Mine* (New York, 1896); society items in San Francisco *Daily Morning Call*, Sept. 20, 1879, Oct. 8-21, 1879; San Francisco *Chronicle*, 1875-1884; San Francisco *Wasp*, 1878.

CHAPTER 16: Adolph Sutro's House

The quotations are from the Sutro family papers in the possession of Mr. Carlo Morbio, Adolph Sutro's grandson.

Additional sources: Eugenia Kellogg Holmes, *Adolph Sutro, a Brief Story of a Brilliant Life* (San Francisco, 1895);

PORTRAITS AND STORIES

George D. Lyman, *Ralston's Ring; idem, Saga of the Comstock Lode* (New York, Charles Scribner's Sons, 1934); C. H. Shinn, *The Story of the Mine*; oral information from Mr. Carlo Morbio.

CHAPTER 17: Two Queens and Their Castles

The quotations are from Ward McAllister, *Society as I Have Found It* (New York, 1890), pp. 243-244; H. H. Bancroft, *History of California*, VII, 545; San Francisco *Chronicle*, Feb. 7, 1872; San Francisco *Alta California*, Mar. 30, 1878; San Francisco *Argonaut*, Jan. 6, Feb. 3, 1883; San Francisco *Chronicle*, Apr. 11, 25, 1887; San Francisco *Examiner*, July 26, 27, 30, 1891.

Additional sources: Bertha Berner, *Mrs. Leland Stanford; an Intimate Account* (Stanford University, Stanford University Press, 1935); Boutwell Dunlap, "Some Facts Concerning Leland Stanford and His Contemporaries in Placer County," *California Historical Society Quarterly*, II (1923), 203-210; Mary Watson, *San Francisco Society, Its Characters and Characteristics* (San Francisco, 1887); Caroline Wenzel, "Finding Facts about the Stanfords," *California Historical Society Quarterly*, XIX (1940), 245-255; San Francisco *Daily Morning Call*, Nov. 4, 1879; society items in San Francisco *News Letter* and *Wasp*, various issues, 1875-1891; conversations with Lucius Booth (a cousin of Newton Booth) about 1900.

For generous help in gathering material for this book the author expresses heartiest thanks to the staff of the Bancroft Library at the University of California, to Miss Ynez Haase, Mr. William Hail, Miss Dorothy H. Huggins, Professor Benjamin H. Lehman, and also to Miss Mary Randall, who shared in many a picture-hunting expedition.

www.ingramcontent.com/pod-product-compliance
Lightning Source LLC
Chambersburg PA
CBHW021710230426
43668CB00008B/790